SEO 2016

learn
SEARCH ENGINE
OPTIMIZATION

R.L. ADAMS

ISBN-10: 1512275069
ISBN-13: 978-1512275063

This Page Intentionally Left Blank

R.L. ADAMS

All Rights Reserved

Legal Notices

The Author was complete as possible in the creation of this book. The contents within are accurate and up to date at the time of writing however the Author accepts that due to the rapidly changing nature of the Internet some information may not be fully up to the date at the time of reading. Whilst all attempts have been made to verify information provided in this publication, the Author assumes no responsibility for errors, omissions, or contrary interpretation of the subject matter herein. Any perceived slights of specific people or organizations are unintentional.

TABLE OF CONTENTS

WHAT IS SEO?

SEO is Search Engine Optimization. It's the set of principles, tools, and techniques used to organically rank content on search engines like Google. And, although SEO might involve a complex set of methods and techniques implemented over time, the core concept is rather simple:

To be successful at SEO, you have to earn trust – Google's trust that is.

In order to illustrate the concept of trust, let's think about the following scenario. You're a new business that just opened up shop and you're looking for a loan from the bank. You have no history of sales or revenue, but you approach the bank for money.

Most people know how this scenario will play out. When you sit down with the banker, he'll ask to review your business's financial statements from the last couple of years. Don't have any business financials to present? How can the banker trust that you'll pay back the money that the bank lends?

Now, think about this bank as being Google and your new business as your Website that you're trying to optimize for SEO. How likely is Google going to trust your new business, or even a business that's been around for a short period? Undoubtedly, its level of trust in you will be limited.

Of course, in the real world, the banker would most likely turn your business down for a loan, unless you were willing to put up collateral or personally guarantee that loan. Unfortunately, in the virtual world, it's not as simple as that. There are no personal guarantees.

So, if Google doesn't trust your site, how can you expect it to send you virtually limitless amounts of organic traffic? Those top few listings are highly coveted. Google knows that the majority of people won't go past that first page.

People simply trust that Google will deliver the most relevant results at the top because it's always done so for them in the past. We all know that those are the most relevant results to our searches, so we're less likely to go beyond those initial results.

Yet, getting to the top is becoming increasingly difficult. And as the Web continues to expand, so does the competitive nature of those coveted first page results. But, we'll peel away that veil of secrecy one layer at a time to expose the truth on just what it takes to get Google to trust you.

Once Google trusts you, and you've exhibited higher trust than your competitors over time, then you'll build relevancy. But, without trust, you can never be deemed relevant, that's why trust is a foundational core concept in SEO.

So, now that we understand we need to be trusted in order for Google to deem us relevant, where do we go from there? How is trust actually built and earned? What are the precise methods and techniques for doing this without violating one of Google's many rules?

Well, that's exactly what you're going to learn in the pages of this book.

So, who am I and why should you listen to me?

My name is R.L. Adams, and I've written some of the best selling books and audiobooks on the topics of SEO and marketing. And I've built up two multi-million dollar businesses using the concepts and techniques that I teach in these very books.

What I've come to realize over time is that, in the business world and in the virtual world, everything revolves around value. No matter what day and age we speak about in history, what you'll realize is that those who deliver more value are those who always rise to the top.

Today, the real world and the virtual world are racing to an inevitable augmentation. The principles that work in the real world are being implemented in the virtual world. Google will trust you and deem you relevant if it sees you consistently delivering an exceedingly high amount of value.

In this book, I'll teach you just how to do that and just

how you can build up Google's trust and succeed with SEO through this value-added approach. I'll teach you what to do and what not to do. I'll illuminate the pitfalls and help to highlight techniques for building trust quicker.

So, if you're ready to take this journey into truly understanding the world of SEO, then let's begin.

1

HOW TO BUILD TRUST

To better illuminate the concept of trust, and how it can be built up over time, or even broken overnight, we first have to understand what the components of trust are. What does Google use to determine a trusted Webpage?

The biggest mistake that people make when approaching SEO is in looking to do the least amount of work for the greatest return. This essentially equates to a non-value-added approach. When, in fact, people need to consider doing the most amount of work for the least initial return.

So, what do I mean by that?

Well, let's first define what a value-added approach is. What does it mean to spread value? On the Web, value is spread with successfully answering a person's question by providing the most well written and well-researched resource available on the topic.

This concept of value presents itself in the content written, video produced, or app created. If value isn't present, then the content will lack something that we call "stickiness." This is easily determined by the amount of time a person spends on a particular Webpage, watching a video, or even using an app.

In the world of SEO, you have to focus on delivering an exceedingly high amount of value if you want to succeed at all. Simply put, you can't do the least amount of work and expect the greatest return. You have to do the greatest amount of work, and initially accept a low return.

I'm illuminating this point because I want you to understand that if you're going to be successful in SEO, you have to deliver value. Don't try to do the least amount of work for the greatest return. If you do, Google simply won't trust you.

So, value comes through content, and that content is one of the factors that Google bases its trust in you. But, what else is involved? Surely, it's not just about value through content? How else is trust built? Well, there are indeed three other important factors when it comes to building trust.

In the proceeding illustration of a pyramid, you'll see the basic building blocks of trust, which include four separate components.

1. **Authority** – A Webpage's authority boils down to its link popularity. That link popularity is made up of several components such as the number of links, the PageRank of those links, the relevancy of those links, and the content it comes from, and

so on.

2. **Age** – Age might be nothing but a number, but to Google age is a critical factor. So, what do I mean by age? Let's think back to that example where Google is the bank and you're the new business going for a loan. In this instance, your age is determined by the initial date that Google indexed your content or Webpage.

3. **Content** – How good is your content? This might sound subjective to you, but Google has algorithms to determine the quality of your prose. Well-researched content that's well written is the basis for providing value and one of the key components for building trust.

4. **Relevancy** – The final piece of the SEO equation is relevancy. How relevant are you to a user's specific search? Relevancy is determined by a number of criteria; it combines both the first three components along with the dimension of similar on-topic content. We'll discuss just what this means.

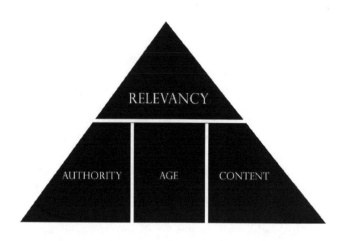

PYRAMID OF TRUST

So we have four components at play here for SEO, three of which largely form the basis for the fourth. Google will trust, and in turn deem you relevant, if it sees you adding value and conforming to its set of rules.

Those rules are vast, and stretch from website design principles to content creation principles, technical guidelines, and of course on-page optimization principles.

But, let's not get overwhelmed here. Let's discuss this one component at a time. Once you understand the components better, we'll dive right into some real-world examples of optimization and even some strategies for building out quality SEO content.

However, before we move forward, let's look at the concept of trust a bit further. Let's explore what it really means to have Google trust you, and just how Google has built this concept of trust through historical references.

In fact, Google wasn't always so stringent in its guidelines of trust. In the past, it was far easier to prop up a Website, build out some content, create some links, and rank on Google's coveted first page relatively quickly. But, then again, the competition was far less fierce and the number of cooks in the kitchen was far less.

Today, that's not the case. Everyone wants to rank at the top of Google's search engine results pages (SERPs). People know that once they can rank at the top of Google's SERPs, they'll enjoy almost limitless free organic search traffic.

Google has built a multi-billion dollar empire around the sheer fact that it has such a far reach. But, Google also knows that some people will do some underhanded things to reach the top of its SERPs. And, this has led to a number of changes that the company has instituted over time to ensure that trust isn't easily achieved.

The changes, also referred to as algorithm adjustments, since they've altered just how Google ranks content on the Web using its search algorithm, have had an enormous impact on the virtual playing field. They've razed and decimated the ranks of some listings, while uplifting the ranks of others.

It's important to look at this information in order to see just what's changed over the years and why it's changed. These changes will add perspective to your understanding of SEO and just what it takes today in order to rank content on Google's coveted SERPs.

ALGORITHM ADJUSTMENTS

The major changes that we've seen in the past have forever altered the search landscape. They've also refined and reshaped just what Google deems as trustworthy with the release of each major update to its search algorithm.

Algorithm adjustments help to provide perspective and a deeper understanding for just where search once was, as opposed to where it is today. With this understanding, you'll have a keen eye for just how to best utilize your time and optimization efforts.

This understanding will also help to drive home what *not to do* when it comes to SEO. What you should keep in mind while reading through the following algorithm adjustments is just how each of them have had an impact on the value of Google's search.

The concept of value is important because Google

knows that in order to maintain its position as the king of all search engines, it must ensure that its organic searches provide the most relevant results in the quickest manner possible.

To Google, this is its value proposition. No other search engine has been able to come close to what Google can provide in the value department. Most people know that if they're searching for something on Google, they're likely to find their answer quickly and at the top of its SERPs.

So, why exactly did Google institute these algorithm adjustments? Well, you've most likely heard of these in the past if you're not already familiar with them. They take on strange names like Panda, Penguin, and Hummingbird.

But, regardless of what they're called, the point remains that the purpose of these adjustments were to ensure that the most relevant results were appearing at the top of its SERPs, and not results that were artificially positioned there by trying to bend or abuse the system.

But in the past that's precisely what was happening. The system was being abused and the quality of Google's SERPs and listings were declining. So, Google decided to wage a war – a digital war for that matter. And, these algorithm adjustments were the equivalent of digital atomic bombs that literally leveled the playing field.

What Hat Will You Wear?

So, what happened exactly and why did it happen? Well, to understand that, I first want to introduce another concept to you that will play an integral role in your SEO career. The question you have to ask yourself is *What Hat Will You Wear?*

Since SEO is divided up into multiple camps, each wearing a particular hat, you'll need to determine just what type of hat you'll wear. There are the Black Hats, the White Hats, and the Gray Hats. Each of these camps follows a different subset of rules for approaching SEO.

- **Black Hats** – The Black Hats don't play by the rules. In fact, they like to bend or even break the rules where they can, and take any and all shortcuts that might exist. They role the dice and hope that their tactics will remain undiscovered by Google.

- **White Hats** – The White Hats follow the rules to the tee. They constantly focus on the long-term goal of adding value and ensuring that they're not trying to institute any techniques that might either be deemed unethical or in violation of one of Google's many rules.

- **Gray Hats** – Somewhere in the middle lay the Gray Hats. They don't break the rules like the Black Hats do, but they see no harm in trying to bend and shape their SEO tactics for maximum advancement and little risk to demotion.

This understanding is important, because it provides some historical context to just how Google's trust has been shaped. The Black Hats were labeled as such because they broke the rules, whereas the White Hats took a very aboveboard approach.

Now, in the past, for a long time, it seemed like the Black Hats were winning. They were instituting tactics that artificially inflated the rank of certain listings on Google's SERPs. In effect, this drove down relevancy because they were "gaming" the system.

When Black Hats gamed the system, everybody was losing other than them. Their content was reaching the top of Google's SERPs, providing them with virtually endless amounts of free organic traffic, while their competitors and the end-users were losing.

As the less relevant listings made their way to the top, competitors who were playing by the rules (White Hats), suffered through a drop in traffic, and a resultant drop in revenue and sales. And the end-users were clicking on less-relevant search results at the top of Google's SERPs, leaving them with a sense of frustration.

Keep in mind that Google's main goal has always been relevancy. It wants to show you the most relevant search result in the quickest manner possible. When the top listings aren't the most relevant, Google's reputation suffers.

Of course, today we know that those top listings are highly coveted. It's not simple to push your way there. You have to actually work at it and earn Google's trust by ensuring that you address all of the many different facets when it comes to optimizing your site and your content.

So, therein lied the problem. Google was losing the battle of relevancy to a group of Black Hats who were manipulating the SERPs. And they were receiving an almost limitless amount of traffic and sales because they knew just how the system worked.

Google realized that it had to do something. It had to take back control of the Web. That's where the algorithm adjustments came into effect. They almost completely altered the search environment, sending some sites shooting to the top, while others almost completely fell off its indexes.

But this didn't all happen at once. These came in waves of algorithm adjustments. The focus in the beginning was on the user's experience. How easy was the site to navigate? How much of the information appeared above the fold? How many ads and external links did the content have?

Google implemented a system for determining the quality of the user experience, and pushed out that algorithm for the first time back on February 23rd, 2011 and dubbed it, "*Google Panda.*" You've more likely than not heard about these so-called Panda Attacks.

PANDA – THE FIRST MAJOR ALGORITHM CHANGE

The Google Panda affected roughly 12% of searches, thus beginning the major shift in the search engine landscape. Google was focusing on quality and user-experience, so it naturally cracked down on thin-content sites, content farms, sites with too many advertisements in proportion to the amount of content, and so on.

Since Google was concerned with a quality user-experience, this was the natural first step in its all-out assault on Web content across the spectrum. It determined an algorithm for evaluating the quality of a site, and it did so with a high degree of precision.

For example, one of the determining factors that the Google Panda looked for was for the amount and quality of content that appeared above the fold. The fold, for those of you who don't know, is the part where browser screens initially cutoff a site when first loaded.

The Website's fold can vary based on screen resolution so Google was able to determine some average pixel sizes. But, what this should tell you is that your concentration on quality content should start as close to the top of your site as possible.

If, for example, you have a lot of ads and a very tall header, your content is going to begin much closer to the fold. If you're a web designer or developer, or you're on that career path, keep this important principle in mind. Keep your content at the top and try not to clutter your site with unnecessary elements at the top.

The Google Panda should also send another very strong message to you by conveying that Google's focus has increasingly become a value-oriented approach. It wants to showcase the Websites at the top of its SERPs that are not only the most relevant, but that also provide the most value.

So, what do we mean by this concept of value? Well, we'll speak about this component in greater detail when we discuss the trust in content component of SEO. But, to summarize here, your content will provide high value when it's well researched, well written, and error free.

You simply can't produce subpar content and expect it to rank high on Google. That just won't happen. You have to take the time and energy to ensure that the content not only answers a question, but also answers it in the best possible manner.

PENGUIN – THE SECOND MAJOR ALGORITHM CHANGE

Google didn't stop with the Panda. It continued its digital onslaught and attack against what it considered as the low-quality Web. On April 24th, 2012, it launched the next in a string of algorithm adjustments called the Google Penguin.

At this point, you had the Black Hats really vying for a place on Google's SERPs. They were trying to figure out which direction Google was heading in after the Panda attacks. But Google kept them guessing. Once it stopped with its user-experience updates in Panda, it started its over-optimization penalties with Penguin.

The Google Penguin really hurt many businesses out there that had done the same techniques and strategies for so long that it really came around to bite them. You see, the businesses that focused on value, content, and user-experience weren't negatively affected by these updates. In fact, they were positively boosted.

But, all told, the Penguin only affected 4% of search results, whereas the Panda hit 12%. But, for the 4% that it did affect, the alterations in search positioning gave them a significant beating. But Google was targeting those that were severely over-optimizing their content.

So, what exactly was Google targeting with the Penguin? Well, the Penguin meant to punish Websites that were engaging in what Google began to dub as Black-Hat SEO, which included things like keyword stuffing, hidden or invisible text, meta-tag stuffing, doorway pages, sneaky redirects, article spinning, and machine translation, to name a few.

But it was also going a bit further beyond that. Google was going after the link schemes that had popped up all over the Web. Link schemes allowed you to create thousands of artificial links using software systems, to portray a more optimized Website.

How did Google determine a link was part of a link scheme? It used a formulaic approach. For example, it analyzed things like link acceleration and link quality.

If a site, for example, went from 10 links one month to 1000 links the next month, and all of those links were using the same one or two keywords keyword, Google knew something was up. Even if the links were coming from diverse Websites, due to the acceleration and quality of those links, Google knew it was time to slap them with the Penguin.

So, Google was targeting sites that were going out of their way to really game the system. This really hurt the Black Hats and sent a very powerful message to the Web:

focus on value. Google wanted to see people delivering the highest value throughout every corner of the Web.

Sites that weren't focused on value, and were in fact focused on trying to bend and break the rules, were penalized. What happened to sites that were penalized? Well, they were sent to Google's Sandbox, a digital no-man's land where sites would experience depressed rankings on SERPs.

We'll get back to a discussion about Google's Sandbox and its implication across a wide range of SEO tactics, a bit later. For now, these algorithm adjustments should drive home the fact that there really remain very few "tricks" that can be used against the search engines to quickly gain rank.

This is important to note because you'll always see some system available for sale by some "expert" who's looking to teach you the newest and best tricks in SEO. Whether it's a software program, an app, or some other stealth technique, it could most likely backfire, so be wary.

When it comes to optimizing your site and your content, you should focus on value. We'll look at the best ways to institute the value-added approach by leveraging the Web's authority sites. These will help you make the biggest gains in the shortest period.

Don't know what an authority site is? That's okay. We'll get to all of that shortly.

HUMMINGBIRD – THE THIRD MAJOR ALGORITHM CHANGE

After the digital dust settled with the first two major overhauls to Google's search algorithm, it wasn't quite done yet. It had a lot more work to do. And, although Google did enact other changes to its algorithm, the third major update really was the Google Hummingbird.

With the Hummingbird, Google focused its efforts on contextual search and the semantics of that search. First taking effect on August 30th, 2013, the Hummingbird helped Google move away from specific keywords and more towards Latent Semantic Indexing (LSI).

LSI is something that's been around for a long time in the field of mathematics. It allows the comparison of words in sentences or phrases based on mathematical computations to come up with similar words or phrases that match the original wording structure.

Over time, Google began to refine its LSI-engines, and ultimately kicked things off with Hummingbird. This was also part of a bid towards increased relevancy. Because, if you were searching for a term like "Best Weight Loss Plans," Google wanted you to find other relevant terms similar to it.

An example of this would be a result such as "Top 10 Diets to Lose Weight Fast." This doesn't match the original keyword search exactly, but it does so semantically. Google now searches out those relevant listings and displays the trusted ones at the top if it can match a highly-trusted near-exact match.

Another way the Hummingbird improved search was by helping to answer questions posed by users. For example, when you write "10 pounds to kilograms," or "what is the weather today," you get an answer at the top of Google's SERPs without having to dig into specific listings.

The importance of the Hummingbird depicts how Google didn't want its users to focus on repeating the same keyword repeatedly in the content in order to rank high. Google wanted its listings to focus on value, and it wants to display the relevant listings to the users searching for that particular information.

In the past, too many people were focusing on things like keyword stuffing. Keyword stuffing, as it might sound, is the over usage of a keyword on a Webpage in an effort to rank higher. This is now considered a Black-Hat SEO technique.

Primarily, keyword stuffing was used in the keyword META tag, which is no longer relevant. The keyword

META tag is now obsolete and Google now defaults to an analysis of the page's content, title and META description to pull information about a particular listing.

So, what's the importance of this update? Well, as you can see, Google is attempting to increase the relevance of its search results. If it can't find a listing matching the exact search term you're looking for, it wants to be able to display a trusted listing that is similar enough to be relevant.

This has certainly clouded the SEO environment. No longer are things so black and white as they used to be. You can't simply determine whether Google will present an exact-matched listing or an LSI-matched listing as it serves up its results. And, of course, Google has done this on purpose.

Google wants people to focus on value, and not aim towards over-optimizing. That's why this contextual search was so important. In fact, it affected 90% of the total searches performed on Google. This is much higher than the 12% Panda affected, and the 4% that Penguin affected.

In fact, the Hummingbird was a complete overhaul to Google's search. Although it affected searches in a subtle way, considering 3.5 billion searches are performed per day on Google, the Hummingbird hits 3.15 billion of those searches. That's a far-reaching impact.

Again, this goes towards Google's main aim in the search industry, which is to provide highly relevant search results in order to answer its users questions quickly. It knows that searches don't want to spend forever looking for the answers.

MOBILEGEDDON – THE FOURTH MAJOR ALGORITHM CHANGE

Before 2015, there were some other changes that were instituted to Google's search algorithm such as the Pigeon, the Payday Loan update, the HTTPS/SSL update, Authorship update, and continued Penguin and Panda releases, but the Mobilegeddon update is one that's particularly noteworthy.

With the Google Pigeon, the company was targeting local search results, claiming that the local algorithm was going to more align with the core algorithm. If you're not familiar with the local search algorithms, it's Google's way of producing locally relevant results to you.

For example, when you search for "Best Chinese Restaurants," Google will identify your location first and display the most relevant results to where you're located.

Google knows that if you're just typing "Best Chinese Restaurants" without adding a location to the end of it, you're likely looking for one close to your present location.

Aside for that one, the SSL update is noteworthy but not major. The SSL update states that Websites with SSL enabled site-wide will rank higher than those that don't have SSL enabled, if all other things are equal. So, having a secured site with SSL will give you an extra little push.

More notably however is this Mobilegeddon update. In late April of 2015, Google announced that it would affect mobile rankings of listings favoring those that were mobile-friendly. This impacted 60% of all searches. But this has much more far-reaching implications.

Since the Web is moving away from the desktop and more towards mobile, tablet, and now wearables, it's clear to see that Websites should no longer just be designed for one screen size. Again, this comes back to the user-experience. How do people on mobile phones and tablets see your site?

Google wants to ensure that your site looks good across devices and not just across different browsers on the same device, such as the desktop. This adds another layer of complexity, but it's a critical one to note. This is going to be an important factor in how you approach your SEO.

You must approach your site and content from a design perspective along with a value perspective. You could spend countless hours writing great content, but if that content isn't properly viewable by people on different devices, then you're going to suffer in the rankings.

Again, this is why historical references are important learning points in the field of SEO. These changes have had wide implications on the search engine landscape. And, if nothing else, it should leave you with a deeper understanding of where we've been and where we're going.

This information will also allow you to tailor your work and keep these important design and quality cues in mind as you engage in SEO. Designing mobile-friendly Websites and content should also be something at the forefront of your mind.

If you're not a Web designer, which is perfectly okay, then ensure that whoever you hire implements a CSS design structure that will work across devices, and not only across different browsers on the same device. This is one of the most important points to keep in mind moving forward.

Google understands that the world is moving away from the desktop. And, by implementing this mobile-friendly search, it's sending a powerful message. Eventually, the concept of the desktop won't exist anymore in the traditional sense, and Google's algorithms are reflecting that.

This is why, when you design your site, you should ensure that you do it so that it's friendly to all devices. I'll highlight some of the best practices in doing this. For example, you could implement an existing CSS system such as Bootstrap that will easily allow you to design your site for multiple devices without much headache or legwork.

2
KEYWORD-DRIVEN WORLD

Before we dive further into the concepts and principles that are driving trust and relevancy on the Web, we first have to build an understanding for keywords. What are keywords? How are they used? And how can you estimate their potential search traffic?

Today, Google's world revolves around keywords. Keywords refer to the word, phrase, or sentence used in online search. A keyword can be a short-tail keyword or a long-tail keyword. The short-tail keywords can be as short as a single word; the long-tail keyword can be as long as a full sentence.

What differentiates the two is search volume and competition. Naturally, single word keywords are going to hold much more competition. But, single word keywords will also be a far less relevant approach to performing your SEO work.

For example, the word "diet" or "insurance" would be

next to impossible to optimize for. Google is using the most trusted listings with the highest PageRank and relevance for those search results. The competition there is fierce.

Even the keyword "weight loss" or "insurance plans," both of which are short-tail keywords, would also be very hard to optimize for. The goal of course is to go after longer specific keywords, or long-tail keywords, because they will hold the highest relevancy for you and the greatest chance of discoverability.

Why is that? Well, in the beginning, your site will be less trusted. Unless you have a domain that's built trust over the years, ranking for shorter keywords will be difficult in the beginning. But, long-tail keywords open up a completely new world of discoverability, even for newcomers.

The difference between a regular keyword and a long-tail keyword is that a long-tail keyword can be four or more words, where the short-tail keyword can be anywhere from a single word to just a few words. In the beginning, your focus should be on long-tail keywords.

Long-tail keywords will help you to build up some initial presence to your site, even if the search volume might be low. Remember, in the beginning, your ability to rank will be severely limited due to Google's Sandbox.

Another important point about short-tail keywords versus long-tail keywords is that although long-tail keywords might have a lower search volume, they do make up a greater portion of Google's daily search activity. 70% of all searches performed are long-tail keyword searches according to Moz.com.

Long-tail keywords are also better at catching people

that are in the later stages of the buying cycle. For example, someone searching for "car tires" might only be browsing, whereas someone searching for "best car tires for a 2010 Honda Accord" is basically ready to hit the buy button.

Can you see the difference here? Think about it yourself. When you search for something on Google with short-tail keywords, you're only browsing. You're looking for information and curious to find data related to your search, but not sure what you want to buy specifically.

But, if you're searching for "best diamond size and clarity for engagement rings," then you're most certainly nearing a decision to purchase. The longer the long-tail keyword is, the more likely you're going to reach those individuals in the buying process.

BRAINSTORMING KEYWORDS

Your first step to conducting any SEO work is to ensure that you've properly brainstormed your keywords. Whether you're doing work on an authority site, or you're doing work on your personal website, brainstorming has to be part of the process every single time.

Why is that? The activity of brainstorming helps to transmute ideas from your subconscious mind to your conscious mind. It helps to build links between obscure ideas that might not have once existed before, with concrete thoughts that can be immediately acted upon.

Brainstorming is also the perfect way to come up with ideas for building out excellent well-researched content. It will involve a small portion of your time, but the returns for your time invested will be well worth it.

So how does this work? Well, if you've never

brainstormed before, here's a crash course for you. Pull out a piece of paper and a pen and put on your thinking cap. Set a timer in front of you for 15 minutes and start writing.

In the center of the paper, write out your main idea. What's the general topic you're looking to write about? Can't think of it? What industry is your business in? What do you sell? If you sell shoes, then in the center of the page, write "Shoes."

Now, even though you sell shoes, that doesn't mean you should restrict your content to only be about shoe sales. Keep in mind that you're trying to target people that want to buy shoes, but you also want to add value to the world in the meantime.

So, what are some ways that you can add value to the world while still promoting or selling your shoes? Well, let's think about the shoe buying process for a moment. What is that process like for men? What's that process like for women?

How does someone go from the idea of a simple shoe, to the thought of buying the right shoe for the right occasion at the right time of the year? Well, let's create some branches on that page. We can come up with several ideas here:

1. Shoe types

2. Shoe colors

3. Shoe gender

4. Shoe size

5. Shoe occasions

6. Shoe seasons

If we were looking for ways to add value, how would we do it? Well, as we're brainstorming, we can see these various ideas when it comes to shoes in front of us. Shoes and the shoe-buying process can be starkly different for men and women.

So, let's think about how this process goes for one or the other. We can take shoe gender and branch off to male or female. For males, how does that buying process work? Do we wake up one day and think about the fact that we need new shoes?

Usually, new shoes, for men at least, are considered when an important occasion is nearing or there's a change in occupation, or their present shoes are simply falling apart. So, how can we help men along this buying process? And how best can we add value at the same time?

Well, from the "males" branch of "shoe gender" we can create a few more branches. Those branches can lead to things like "new jobs," "life events," "seasons," and "vacations."

When we see these branches in front of us, and think about the process in this manner, it helps to uncover hidden possibilities that might not have been apparent to us before.

Now that we've done some brainstorming on shoes, and we've thought about the shoe-buying process, how can we create a few long-tail keywords to summarize our research? Well, here are a few thoughts and ideas of what we can do.

1. Best dress shoes for men

2. Best winter shoes for men

3. Best hiking boots for men

4. Best formal shoes for men

5. Best beach sandals for men

The list uses the word "best" in all five long-tail keywords. Why use a word like *best*? Well, when we're searching for the best of something, we're generally ready to buy. We could be searching for the best hairdresser, the best car wash, the best gardener, and so on.

We search using the word best when we are ready to take some action and make a purchase. We wouldn't just search for the words "dress shoes," we would want to qualify that search if we were serious about it. We might even do something like "Best dress shoes for men under $100."

You get the idea right? That's why long-tail keywords and the brainstorming process are so important. It helps you to uncover ideas like this that you might not have had before. We could use other words to qualify our search in long-tail keywords as well.

We could use words like "top," or "cheapest," or "highest rated," and so on. We're using these words to qualify our search in long-tail keywords because we're ready to make our purchase. Get the idea? It's rather straightforward, but does involve some thought on your part.

Of course, the list can go on and on here. But you

should come up with 5 or 10 different options that involve long-tail keywords. Once you have your brainstorming session complete and your long-tail keywords, you can head over and start the balance of your research.

When you're brainstorming your keywords, keep in mind that you don't have to come up with just one idea. You can branch out and think about your business or your topic from multiple perspectives, and not just a sales perspective.

For example, you might want to think about the industry that you're in. In this case, it would be the apparel industry. You might also want to think about the customer demographic whoever that might be. You can also think about the sales climate, or the leading distributors in the business.

This could lead to multiple scenarios that you might not have thought about from the outset. It could lead to doing research into the sales cycle of shoes, where they're most typically purchased from, how much someone typically spends on them, and so on.

You can use this data to put together a nice infographic, a video tutorial, or some other how-to guide. Don't be afraid to go out there and explore, even if you're moving off on a tangent. That's the great part about brainstorming.

The unfortunate truth is that most people skip this step entirely. I wouldn't recommend doing that at all. If you're going to write a post that adds value, and not just one that wants to sell something to someone, you have to brainstorm the ideas first.

The mind has a funny way of transmuting subconscious thoughts onto paper when it's ready to do so. If you simply think about concepts in the abstract, and don't actually apply the act of brainstorming, you might never come up with a brilliant idea that will lead to tons of traffic.

Remember, your goal here is to add value. Google wants to see you adding an exceedingly high amount of value in whatever you do. Don't be afraid to dig your heels in, do the research, and put some considerable thought and effort into what you want to write about.

Even if you're writing an article about the "best dress shoes for men," you won't just be trying to sell shoes. You will literally seek out and find the best and highest-rated dress there are for me. Compare and contrast them. What sets them apart? What the positives and negatives of both?

You see, you're adding value. And, if you're in the shoe business, then you're most likely an authority on shoes. So, writing out a list of the "best dress shoes for men" shouldn't be a major hurdle for you. You're adding value to the world and selling will just be a secondary notion.

BRAINSTORMING WITH GOOGLE TRENDS

A great tool to use while brainstorming for your keyword ideas is to use Google Trends. This helps bring insight into what people are searching for out there. You can find trends by year, by country, by topic, by people, by image, and so on.

You can use Google Trends to see what's been popular in the last year when it came to searches in your field or industry. Which searches made it to the top of the list? Can that give you some insight into what people are interested in finding out?

Google Trends isn't the only answer to your brainstorming needs, but it can help to stimulate the mind to think about areas that you might not have considered before. It's also a great tool to use when you're looking to create content that is time-sensitive and you want to rank now.

Often, you might find Google Trends for keywords that presently have a low search competition but a high search volume. This is a great way to appear relevant at the top since not many people were vying for that search term in the past.

If you can combine a Google Trend with a long-tail keyword, then that's even better. You have to get creative at times in order to push the envelope and find ways to do things that you might not have thought of earlier in the game.

So, use this tool to scour out some additional avenues of content that you might consider distributing out there. If nothing else, it should help to get the juices flowing to enhance your brainstorming activities.

To use Google Trends, simply head to: google.com/trends where you can explore the many varieties that Google gives you for discovering what's hot in search now and in the past. This should give you a general idea on where search trends might be heading, and allow you to capitalize on that by building out some great high-value, unique content.

RESEARCHING KEYWORDS

Researching doesn't end with brainstorming. In fact, it just begins. The goal for brainstorming is to come up with an array of ideas that can be used while researching keywords. When we talk about research, we're actually referring to the hard numbers.

What does that mean? Well, what we want to find out is just how popular a given search term is going to be. How many people are searching for your long-tail keyword? Is there heavy competition, or is it marginal?

Now, the tool used for doing this is called the Keyword Planner Tool and it comes from the search giant itself. But, the Keyword Planner Tool is really a tool that is meant for advertisers that are looking to place ads on Google's network, so it has its limitations.

However, even though it's a tool for advertisers, it does

offer some of the best insights into searches being conducted on Google in real-time. Specifically, the important insights lay within the competition field and search volumes.

When you conduct a search using the Keyword Planner Tool, Google presents you with a variety of results along with the level of competition and the number of global monthly searches. It can also present you with a number of similar search results.

So let's see just how this works. Point your browser to adwords.google.com/KeywordPlanner or simply Google "Keyword Planner Tool" and click on the first result. When you get to the screen, it will ask you to sign into your Adwords account.

If you don't have an Adwords account, you can set one up. It won't cost you anything. But you will need a Google account to get this going. When you get to the Keyword Planner page, you'll have four different options on what to do next:

1. Search for new keywords and ad group ideas

2. Get search volume for a list of keywords or group them into ad groups

3. Get traffic forecasts for a list of keywords

4. Multiple keyword lists to get new keyword ideas

Keyword Planner
Plan your next search campaign

What would you like to do?

> ‣ Search for new keyword and ad group ideas

> ‣ Get search volume for a list of keywords or group them into ad groups

> ‣ Get traffic estimates for a list of keywords

> ‣ Multiply keyword lists to get new keyword ideas

Now, since we've already done our research and we've created a list of long-tail keywords, we would select the second option on the list "Get search volume for a list of keywords or group them into ad groups." This will allow us to just copy and paste our brainstorming keywords into the Keyword Planner.

But you can also select the first option if you want to start a search from scratch. For example, if you want to search for new keywords, you could find out what Google has in mind or would suggest to you. The first option will allow you to use a variety of targeting methods for your keyword, which are rather self-explanatory.

For now, let's focus on the second option. After clicking on it, you'll find a box for entering in your keywords. You can enter them in one line at a time, or by using commas to separate each keyword. You could also upload a CSV file of a list of keywords if you're so inclined.

The other options include targeting and date range.

These are pre-filled in for you, but you could modify those selections. For example, the default is targeting all locations. But you could target only a specific location, if you're offering a local service for example.

The negative keywords option is only something to consider if you're actually running ads on Google. Why is that? Well, when you advertise on Adwords, you have the option of doing broad matches, phrase matches, or exact matches.

Depending on the type of match you're performing, you could receive paid search traffic that doesn't apply to your offerings. In this case, you can use negative keywords to avoid that from happening. But, since we're focusing on organic search and specific long-tail keywords here, you don't have to worry about that now.

I would recommend initially leaving all targeting options at their default selections, and simply pasting in your list of long-tail keywords. Now, what you might find is that you get zero results for your long-tail keywords. Why is that?

Well, keep in mind that this tool is meant for advertisers on Google's Adwords platform. It's not meant as a way to get the search volume and competition for every single keyword. This is the drawback behind the system. In the past, it was far easier to see search volumes and competition, but all that has now changed.

You can, of course, shorten your keywords to estimate traffic for short-tail keywords, but that won't help you in your approach to SEO. Your focus should remain on long-tail keywords. Focus on phrases and sentences that you think would be popular questions in your field.

But, let's say for a moment that we don't get any results

when we paste in our long-tail keywords. What else can we do? Well, we can continue brainstorming to come up with new ideas, or even start to type keywords into Google's search bar so that we can see them from its autosuggestion tool.

You've undoubtedly used the autosuggestion many times in the past. When you begin to type in "best dress shoes" for example, and hit the space bar, you're presented with a number of the top suggestions for searches that are being performed on Google for this particular term.

Unfortunately, these are not ordered by the most searches down to the least searches. No, Google keeps us guessing with that. But, we could type these terms into the Keyword Planner Tool to complete our research. So, as you can see from the following list, here's what we get when we type in "best dress shoes" then add a space to see what Google suggests.

1. Best dress shoes (short-tail keyword)

2. Best dress shoes for men (long-tail keyword)

3. Best dress shoes for plantar fasciitis

4. Best dress shoes for flat feet

5. Best dress shoes under 200

6.   Best dress shoes for walking

As you can see by the list that we generated using Google's autosuggestion tool, there are plenty of options for writing great content. Additionally, it might present you with ideas that you might not have considered earlier during your brainstorming session.

For example, number three on the list talks about "Plantar Fasciitis," or "Jogger's Heel," a condition that develops as a result of usually over-exercising, from weight, or age.

We certainly see an idea here for writing a post that contains massive value by not only breaking down this ailment, but also in analyzing shoes from this perspective. Which dress shoes for men are the best for those afflicted with jogger's heel?

The fourth result talks about flat feet. That's another great idea for a post. What are the best dress shoes for men who have flat feet? These long-tail keywords are excellent for ranking quickly on Google's SERPs. But, the content has to be great, so always keep that in mind.

Now, getting back to our original list, let's first see what kind of results we come up with. Remember, autosuggestion is a great tool to use if your original list brings back no results. But, our original list will have some results. So, just to remind you, here's what we had before.

1.   Best dress shoes for men

2.   Best winter shoes for men

3. Best hiking boots for men

4. Best formal shoes for men

5. Best beach sandals for men

When we conduct our search using the long-tail keywords through the Keyword Planner, our results indicate the number of monthly searches being performed, plus the level of competition.

For the search results, we can see that through the Keyword Planner that "Best dress shoes for men," is a relatively popular search with around 1,900 searches per month and high competition. This was reinforced by Google's autosuggestion.

Again, the competition level applies to advertisers that are looking to buy ads for this keyword. Still, it does give you a sense of the search volume and how competitive searches are for this long-tail keyword search.

Although high competition here doesn't necessarily equate to high competition in organic search results, the two usually end up being relatively similar.

The understanding here is that advertisers that are looking to compete heavily on certain keyword searches through Google's Adwords, are doing so because the organic search is also very competitive and hard to rank for. For this reason, advertisers are also going after paid search.

Keyword (by relevance)		Avg. monthly searches ?	Competition ?	Suggested... ?	Ad impr. s... ?	Add to plan
Best dress shoes for men	↳	1,900	High	$0.86	–	✓
Best hiking boots for men	↳	1,600	High	$0.80	–	»
Best winter shoes for men	↳	210	High	$1.26	–	»
Best formal shoes for men	↳	140	High	$0.30	–	»
Best beach sandals for men	↳	30	High	$0.58	–	»

However, this still hinders our ability to truly have x-ray vision into Google's results. How are we supposed to work on optimizing keywords and searches for long-tail keywords, when we don't know precisely how competitive organic searches are as opposed to paid searches?

Unfortunately, Google doesn't provide a tool for allowing us to peer into the inner workings of their organic search. That's the core reason why Google is, well, Google. Some things simply can't be revealed to the public for fear of abuse to the system.

As you now know, Google already went through a major ordeal to clean up its SERPs due to Black-Hat SEOs and thin-content sites that were primarily seeking to rank by utilizing virtually any means that were available to them.

For that reason, and many other reasons, Google just doesn't want to reveal too much. However, we can use other tools to glean some more information from Google's SERPs. Although, in a perfect world, Google would be more transparent, there are some next-best solutions.

One of those next-best solutions is the SEO Quake Plugin tool. I've spoken about this tool before in the past and I believe in it a great deal. It's an excellent resource for determining your chances of ranking for a particular keyword search by displaying some important information.

The information that SEO Quake reveals allows us to get a better sense of a Webpage's authority and age, two of the core components in Google's pyramid of trust.

SEO QUAKE PLUGIN

The SEO Quake Plugin helps people peer into Google's search results to see what's going on behind the scenes. This is helpful from a trust perspective because it displays just how Google sees the listings on its SERPs.

We can leverage this information by conducting searches on Google for our long-tail keywords, then analyzing the search results. I'll show you just how to determine how difficult it will be to rank for a particular search using this exact method.

So how does this work?

Well, the first step is to download and install the SEO Quake Plugin tool. However, one quick suggestion – I don't recommend doing this on your primary browser. For example, if you use Chrome as your primary browser, download and install this on Firefox. If you use Firefox, do it on Chrome, and so on.

Ensuring that you don't use this on your primary browser is important. SEO Quake adds extraneous data into every search that you conduct on Google, and sometimes slows your searches down. It's great for the purpose of keyword research, but not so great for everyday usage.

Now, let's head back and conduct those long-tail keyword searches while using the SEO Quake Plugin tool. But, what information, particularly, is this tool going to give us? Well, it's going to show us just how trusted Google deems a particular listing.

Also, a note before you start – you can turn on and off different settings for the SEO Quake Plugin tool from the preferences menu for the extension in the browser. After using the tool on a few searches, you might come to find certain factors more important than others.

When we conduct a search for the first one of our long-tail keywords, namely – "Best dress shoes for men" – we get a set of results that displays standard SERP listings. In the result set, we can see the listings, but also under each listing we see a bar with some statistics and data.

We can see the PR, or PageRank of a page, its Alexa Ranking, the number of Twitter Tweets to the domain, number of Facebook shares for that page, number of Google Plus Ones for that page, and also link to some Whois data to help us determine the site's age.

The top five listings, which are displayed in the proceeding image, can give you an indication of the difficulty to rank for this long-tail keyword. One important thing to note here is that Google will type out the words used to fetch its results in bold format.

So, when we're looking at the top result, for example, we can see that the title is "Men's Shoes Spring 2015 - Best Dress and Casual ..." The description has bold lettering for the words "best men's shoes." It's clear that Google is using these main words to fetch these results.

You can also see the bold letters for the words in the link itself. Google is highlighting the words "mens-shoes" in that first link. But, let's see what else is important here. We can see the PageRank identified by the PR Symbol with a number next to it.

Now, the PR here refers to the PageRank of that particular page, and not of the entire site. We see that the first listing has a PR of N/A, and so do the second and third listings, which is almost the same as 0, and the fourth has a PR of 4, while the fifth has a PR of 5.

Now, how is it that a PR of N/A (or zero) is ranking above a PR of 4? Also, how is that a PR of 4 is ranking above a PR of 5? This is where the over 200 factors in Google's new Post-Hummingbird world come into play in its online search.

If you take a closer look at the first listing, you'll see that it has an Alexa ranking of 3505, symbolized by the "a" icon. The Alexa ranking is a categorization of all of the Websites on the Internet into chronological order. With Alexa, number 1 is the most popular site in the world, and the numbering goes up from there.

What you'll also see here is that the third listing has an Alexa ranking of 3182, which is higher than the ranking of the first listing at 3505, yet it remains in the third position. You can also see that it has 662 Facebook shares of that page as opposed to the number one spot's paltry 7 shares.

What else can we see here? Well, one of the major factors that comes into play when we're discussing authority are the number of links to a page and to the domain. You can see these by turning on the "SEMRush Links" and "SEMRush Linkdomain" parameters in the preferences for SEO Quake.

The "L" and the "LD" for links to the page and links to the domain represent those two pieces of information, respectively. The reason listing number 1 is appearing before 3, even though the PageRank is nominal or non-existent for both has to do with the other factors that are involved.

Why?

As we can see, listing number three has more links to its domain. In fact, it has 666,931 links to its domain as opposed to 288,322 for listing number one. Now, you can imagine that the competition here is fierce and you'll be hard-pressed to rank for this organic search.

But, what still remains to be seen is why listing number one is ranking ahead of listing number three? Well, in this instance, age is most likely the deciding factor. Since the content is thin on both sites, the other trust factors come into play in order to help provide the deciding factor.

One piece of information that you can't garner from these listings is just how good the content is that's written on the listings respective pages. Unless of course you go read each listing's content, which might pose as useful to you, you'll be unable to determine how good they are.

Of course, another piece of very useful information is the Whois data, which will tell us the domain's age. As you'll recall, domain age is just one of the trust components involved in the pyramid of trust that Google relies on to help rank listings.

Listing number one was registered in 1994, whereas listing number three was first registered in 1995. As you can see by all of this, SEO Quake can prove to be a very useful tool for us as we're conducting our SEO activities and determining whether we can rank for a particular search.

So, what does that tell us about this search? Well, Google is using Hummingbird here to find similar listings that it already trusts, since it's not displaying any listings that match this exact long-tail keyword search. What this also tells you is that you have a small chance to rank on the first page of Google's SERPs for this long-tail keyword.

The competition for this search is fierce, because as you move down the list, you'll see that each of the SERP listings have a huge number of links going to their domains, making them incredibly popular. Unless you dish out an extraordinary piece of content on an authority site, ranking for this search will be hard.

So, what are you supposed to do?

Well, your next task is to try conducting your SEO Quake research using the autosuggestions as well. What do the top results look like for those searches? What are your chances of ranking high for one of Google's autosuggestions that you uncovered?

This isn't an exact science by any means, but it is a way to make an educated guess on where to spend your time. Keep in mind that the content writing is going to be an exhaustive endeavor for you, so be sure that your limited resource of time is focused in the right direction.

3

TRUST THROUGH AUTHORITY

One of the core concepts and principles to SEO is that of authority. What is authority? How is it built? And who gets to define what authority really means? Well, let's think about the word itself first. What does it mean to have authority and who can actually command it?

If we think about the business world, someone like the president or chief executive officer of a company would wield authority. They're in a position of power because they worked to get to that level. They either started the business or worked their way up over time.

The same concept applies in the entertainment world. Who has commanding authority there? Well, producers and directors for one, but also well-known actors. How did they get there? Through hard work and dedication. It didn't happen overnight.

We also see this concept in sports. Sport stars have authority in their given profession. From basketball, to football, soccer, baseball, and hockey, no matter what sport we talk about, the players are the authorities there. They've built up their skills over years and years of practice and hard work.

So, authority is something that's built up over time, right? Well, yes, exactly. And that means that if your Website is brand new, you're going to be lacking authority. So, why is this important? Well, Google won't trust you if you lack authority.

All of this boils down to trust. Let's think back to the original example again of the new business that goes to a bank for a loan. The bank officer asks for some business credentials such as past years tax returns or income statements, but there are none to produce because it's a new business.

How likely is that new business to get a loan? Not likely at all, unless of course there's a personal guarantee from a director, principle, or officer. In that case, sure, the bank would likely extend a loan depending on the creditworthiness of the individual making the personal guarantee.

However, in the SEO world, it doesn't work quite as simply as that. Authority is something that's built up over time, and not something that happens overnight. This is also why Websites that have been around for a long time (i.e. 3+ years) always rank higher on Google's SERPs.

Websites that have been around for a long time, and have steadily built up authority by creating meaningful content and getting meaningful links from other trusted sites on the Web, will always appear higher up on the SERPs.

In a way, Google created this all-important limiting

factor for a particular reason. It's not easy to climb up the SERPs any longer without authority, and it's impossible to built authority unless it's done so over time. So, authority is something that's earned, not overnight, but steadily over years.

So, where does that leave us? How are we supposed to do SEO when we lack authority? Well, that topic certainly warrants a discussion. But to summarize for now, authority is going to be built by leveraging existing authority sites and other niche websites to create high-value content that then links back to your own unique high-value content.

Sound like a lot of work? Well it is! No one said that SEO was going to be easy. Be prepared to dig your heels in and grind away.

UNDERSTANDING PAGERANK

In the early days, when Google was coming up with its algorithm to help index the Web, it created something called PageRank. PageRank can be clearly defined by a formula that conveys a level of importance, from zero to ten, to any given page on the Web.

But, what is PageRank exactly? How does the formula work? Simply put, it boils down to a computation that can index a site or particular Webpage by its likeliness to randomly appear in search. Its PageRank is a numerical representation of that formula.

$$PageRank \ of \ site = \sum \frac{PageRank \ of \ inbound \ link}{Number \ of \ links \ on \ that \ page}$$

OR

$$PR(u) = (1 - d) + d \times \sum \frac{PR(v)}{N(v)}$$

The formula for PageRank is a number generated by Google that tallies the value of a particular page in relation to all the other sites on the Web. Now, this isn't the same thing as relevance. Relevance is more like the key to SEO, whereas PageRank is likened to the lock.

A door can exist with a lock, but it can't be opened without SEO. Of course, the door itself in this analogy is likened to the site itself. Anyone can open a door, but not many people can open a locked door without a key.

Another important note about PageRank is that each step up in the ladder is exponentially greater than the step before it. For example, moving from a PageRank of 3 to a PageRank of 4 might sound simple, but in fact it's monumentally difficult. Moving from 4 to 5 becomes even harder, and so on.

Websites with a PageRank of 10 are household names such as Google, YouTube, and Facebook. While a PageRank of 9 would be equivalent to a news site such as CNN.com, and on down the list. This is an important concept to understand as it helps to put perspective to the varying of sites out there and what PageRank is attributed to them.

As you can see in the following image depicted here of PageRank done by Elliance, Inc. way back in 2006, it helps to indicate the level of difficulty involved with moving up this so-called mountain that we call PageRank on the Web. In the image, you'll understand the monumental task of going from 5 to 6 let alone moving from 9 to 10.

Of course, PageRank doesn't paint the entire picture. PageRank is simply the formula that determines the importance of a page on the Web. The key to SEO really lies in relevancy. But, even if your content is highly relevant, without a high PageRank, you can't expect great results.

So, we'll discuss just how to build up PageRank in order to have your content relevantly appear in front of the eyes of countless individuals that are looking for your content. There are specific techniques that you can implement, which I will show you in the pages of this book, to increase your PageRank.

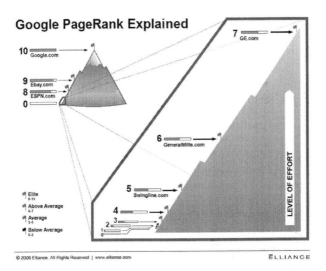

Once your PageRank climbs, appearing relevant in Google's SERPs becomes far easier. But, until that happens, you can expect to get marginal results at best. That is also why we'll leverage authority sites to drive traffic to your content even before your PageRank has climbed to a respectable number.

So, the goal, in order to increase PageRank, is to naturally increase the amount of quality links to your site. And I stress the word *quality*. Links coming from sites that have a high PageRank will outweigh those coming from

R.L. ADAMS

low PageRank sites. But it doesn't end there.

In order to build PageRank, you have to ensure you adhere to the following steps. These steps will help you to build authority over time, and thus increase your PageRank. Keep in mind that the formula for PageRank relates to the number and quality of inbound links to your site.

Your goal to increase your site's PageRank will involve the following steps:

1. Build content that has value

2. Create authority site content

3. Create links to your content

4. Develop relationships with bloggers

5. Engage in real conversations

STEP #1 – BUILD CONTENT THAT HAS VALUE

The absolute first step in increasing your PageRank and authority on the Web is to ensure that you create high-value content. Remember, there are millions upon millions of people vying for those coveted top spots on Google's SERPs, so what's going to set you apart?

Whether your site is new or old, you have to focus on content. If you've heard the expression before, *Content is King*, there's no truer statement. This has a great deal to do with Google's desire to make the Web a more valuable resource.

It's no longer okay to simply throw together content and expect it to rank high. Unless you're a serious authority out there in your niche, you're going to have to work incredibly hard to build up your PageRank by consistently writing excellent content.

Even if your site has some authority, the content must still deliver enormous amounts of value. The fact remains that Websites don't become authorities by simply posting subpar content. So, focus on creating excellent unique, well-written content that you spend the time to research.

We'll get into strategies involving creating excellent well-written content that provides an exceedingly high amount of value. Now, keep in mind that I can't write this content for you. But I will give you pointers and best practices on how you can do this with less friction.

When you set out to create this content, you'll also need to keep some principles in mind regarding on-site optimization, something we'll get into in the coming chapters and sections. For the time being, ensure that you do your research and brainstorm the topics that would best fit your niche.

Keep in mind that you want to create focused content that targets your niche, and of course, that adds an exceedingly high amount of value to the world. You don't want to write a review for a laptop on a site focused on healthcare. You have to be niche-specific with your content.

This concept of being niche specific is important in the SEO industry. In fact, Google likes to see sites that focus on a specific niche and don't veer off course too much from their general focus. This also helps to build authority in your particular niche, while not trying to be a jack-of-all-trades.

So, the best thing to do is to consider just what you want to write about by engaging in some productive brainstorming sessions. If you've never brainstormed before, now is the time to hone those skills because what you write about is going to either help you or hinder you.

In SEO, you have to be a jack-of-all-trades, so to speak. Not only do you have to be technically savvy, but you also have to have skills in areas like design, social media, and writing. What you'll come to find out is that you'll have to engage in a wide range of practices to excel, so be prepared to learn what you don't yet understand.

Set out on paper what you think would be the best possible things you could offer to help to educate the general public in your niche or market. What can you teach them? Remember, this content has to have an exceedingly high amount of value. It can't simply be something you throw together.

It must also always be error-free, and not laced with grammatical or spelling problems. Google will penalize you for that. So, if you don't want to be at more of a disadvantage than you already are when you start out, take the time to prepare something great.

This is content that you'll publish on your personal site or the site of your client's. It can be a how-to article, a video tutorial, or some other piece of content that helps to answer a question or fill a need. But it has to be content of high value! I can't stress that point enough.

STEP #2 – CREATE AUTHORITY SITE CONTENT

Once you've created your excellent piece of content on your site, your next step will be to create a similar excellent piece of content on an authority site. Yes, I know, you have to do the work twice. But why is that? Well, as you now know, authority sites have a built-in trust with Google.

Authority sites not only have a high PageRank, but they also have one other unique feature. And that feature is that they allow you, me, and anyone else who wants to, to post content there freely and willingly without having to pay for it.

That content will rank far quicker on Google's SERPs than any content that you post on your site. That's because Google already trusts these sites. They've been around for years and years, some of them for decades. You simply can't compete with that.

Authority sites have also built up their authority over time with Google. They have hundreds of thousands, if not millions of links back to their various pages throughout the Web. Google trusts these sites implicitly.

So, your job now, once you've created some excellent content and posted it on your Website, is to do it again. I spoke about this strategy in a book called *SEO Strategies & Techniques*, which is part of the *SEO University Series* of books that I released in the not-so-distant past.

If you're serious about advanced SEO strategies, I would suggest that you check it out. But, regardless, I'll give you a breakdown of just how and why this strategy works to increase authority and PageRank. If you'll recall, PageRank is a formula that takes into account link popularity.

In effect, PageRank is the sum of the popularity of your links, and the quality of those links. By quality, we mean how many more links out from that page are there where your link is coming from? Is that page linking to dozens of sites, or just yours? Is it a "dofollow" link or a "nofollow" link?

Sound confusing? Well, in tech-speak, a "dofollow" link is a link that Google will follow if its spiders see it. A "nofollow" link is a link that Google will not follow. When there are many links to other sites on your page, it's good practice to add the "nofollow" attribute to them.

Now, although PageRank isn't the full formula for ranking, relevancy drives that factor home. Relevance is achieved through the three trust components, but relevant content is the key here to ensure you increase your PageRank. Linking two relevant pieces of content is going to be critical.

To illustrate this concept, I wanted to show you a graphical depiction of this and just how this works. You're going to get the greatest benefit from building out content in this manner, than you will by using any other strategy, so pay careful attention.

In the first step, we created high-value content on your Website. In this second step, we're creating high-value content on an authority site. But which authority sites are we using? Well, we can use several, but just to name a few, let's try the following:

- Blogger.com

- HubPages.net

- Scribd.com

- Slideshare.net

- Tumblr.com

- Vimeo.com

- Wordpress.com

- YouTube.com

The PageRanks of these Websites are very high. Now, I know what you're thinking – you already have a blogger or Wordpress site setup on your custom domain, why do you have to setup another one? Well, this is different. This isn't on your personal domain. This is on the Wordpress or Blogger domain.

Both of those sites have options where you can build

out a blog with a subdomain, and that's the option that you should choose. For example, you could setup the following blogs at mygreatbusiness.wordpress.com or abcwidgets.blogger.com.

What you want to do is ensure that you're using those domains from blogger.com or wordpress.com because they have high authority. When you post on those blogs, they also spread the links through the domain itself with new posts, and there are techniques to get more exposure in that way, too.

Content Marketing

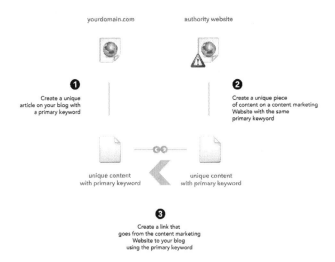

This authority-building strategy actually falls under the realm of content marketing, because that's what you're doing, in effect. You're marketing existing content on your Website with similar content on an authority site.

In the image, you'll see this graphically depicted. On the one side, we have the content on your domain. On the other side, we have the content on the authority domain. Both pieces of content are highly unique and create value. But the authority content has a single link to your content.

Why is this so important? Well, it's that single, solitary link that's going to build up your PageRank and resultant authority. And that link must be through the keyword that you're targeting. Of course, we'll get into greater detail on this later, but I wanted to highlight this now early on as a summary.

When high-value content on an authority site links to high-value content on your domain through a targeted keyword, your site's PageRank increases. But this also increases the relevancy of your content for that keyword search.

You're much more likely to be found now through that keyword for a search than you were before. Plus, your authority content will likely be found before content is found on your domain, so this is a win-win situation. Yes, it requires a lot of work, but it's very worthwhile.

STEP #3 – CREATE LINKS TO YOUR CONTENT

Since PageRank is all about authority building, and authority building is all about creating quality links back to your content, the next natural step is to create links to your content. And I'm not talking about the single solitary link that goes from the authority-site content to your domain's content.

Creating links to your content is all about finding quality sites that you can use to begin building up the link presence of your content. Today, this includes social media sites and other sites of notable presence. Of course, this must be done with decorum.

So, how do we go about this? Well, this is rather straightforward and simple. What you want to do is to create as many quality links back to your content and to the authority content that's linking back to your content, as you possibly can.

Sharing the link through social media and other avenues on the Web helps to achieve this goal. Keep in mind that you want to do this with tact. For example, on Facebook, it's best to setup a Facebook Page for the content that you'll be sharing rather than sharing it personally.

Now, although this will get you less exposure, it's about the quality of the link, and also not enraging your friends and followers by constantly bombarding them with links that they might not care too much to see posted repeatedly on your personal page.

With a Facebook Page or Google Plus Page, you can hone your content to your niche, and build a fan-base and followers in that arena and gear it towards building audience for your business. If you're an SEO professional, then this is something that you'll need to do for clients.

Why is this so important? Well, those links are integral to the success of your content, the PageRank of your site, and the probability that you'll be deemed relevant for those particular searches. Without spreading the links, there's no way you can increase your PageRank.

Now, one other quick concept that I want you to keep in mind here is that of the Google Sandbox. If you'll recall, the Google Sandbox is where Google places sites that are misbehaving. That virtual playground really is no fun at all.

But, the Google Sandbox also acts as a virtual filter for new Websites. This is due to Google's lack of trust for the newbies. If your site is new, in that Google hasn't indexed your site more than 2 years ago, then the power of links going to your site will also be subdued.

So, what do we mean by the power of links? Well, each link holds a particular weight to it. Very important links from high PageRank Websites are said to hold considerable link juice. Link juice is just another way of referring to the power of a link.

When your site is new, in that Google only recently indexed it within the last two years, the link juice coming from links will be subdued because they will be filtered by Google's Sandbox. There's simply no way around this.

The fact remains that you're just going to have to do the work, and over time, your PageRank and your authority will increase. This is also why you'll want to build authority-site content. Your authority-site content will get exposure far before content on your personal domain does.

When you create links, you'll want to create links to both pieces of content by sharing them through as many avenues as you can. As long as the content is excellent, well written, and it adds value, then it's most likely something that people will share themselves.

As other users share your content, your authority and your PageRank will increase, but it won't happen overnight. This is one of the most frustrating components about SEO – it takes hard work applied over an extended period.

No matter what anyone tells you, there is no magic bullet. Special software, stealthy apps, or other shortcuts aren't going to do it. You have to put in the blood, sweat, and tears. It will take you time, but eventually, you will succeed.

In the meantime, you'll have your authority site content that will get you some relevant search traffic. If you understand the principles of marketing, then you can also use that authority-site content to sell things to people, as long as it doesn't come across as a hard sell.

What do I mean? Well, when you build out your authority site content, you're doing so from a perspective of adding value to the world. But, that doesn't mean you can't finish off your piece of content with a statement to contact you or your company for similar services or products.

For example, if you take the time to build out a lengthy post on how to write a the perfect resume, including the best tips and practices, pitfalls, interview techniques, and so on, you could close that post with a soft sell on how they can hire a professional to write their resume for them.

Of course, by a professional, you mean you, if you're selling resume-writing services, that is. Add your phone number, an email address, and some basic information on what a resume would cost them. For example, "Contact us to get a professional resume without all the hassle for as little as $99."

Now, where are we supposed to post or share links to our content once it's written? What are the best sites to use in order to do this? Well, there are so many social media sites these days, but only a few important ones, and probably even less very important ones. Here's a list to use:

1. Twitter.com (PageRank: 10) – Twitter is a great place to share your content. If you have experience using Twitter, then that's great. If not, that's okay too. Setup a Twitter account and get to know the system and how it's used. Then, when you post content, ensure that you share the link of both content on your domain and content from

the authority domain on Twitter. Use relevant hashtags in order to target that content to the right audience.

2. Facebook.com (PageRank: 9) – Of course, we all know the importance of Facebook and its role in today's increasingly social online environment. If you haven't already setup a Facebook Page for your business, product, or service, now is the time to do so. You'll be sharing links here for your fans or friends, and you'll use this tool to help increase your site's PageRank steadily over time.

3. Plus.Google.com (PageRank: 9) – While Google Plus might not be at the forefront of everyone's mind, it's certainly a site with a high PageRank where content should be shared and shared often. Like Facebook, you can setup a business page on Google Plus and use it to share your content. Again, you'll be sharing links to your personal site and to authority site content here. Although Google Plus holds no more importance in Google's algorithm just because it's a Google service, it does have a high PageRank, so make sure you're using it.

4. LinkedIn.com (PageRank: 9) – Another popular place to share your content is through LinkedIn. Most people already have a LinkedIn profile setup and have used it in the past. But, this is another great avenue for sharing content. LinkedIn's high PageRank and authority make it the perfect place

to gain exposure for both your Website and for your authority-site content.

5. Xing.com (PageRank: 9) – Similar to LinkedIn, this is a social network geared towards business professionals around the world, and has approximately 13 million users and climbing. This is another great avenue to help share your links in a diversified environment. Google likes to see diversity in link sharing, and not to see the same sites linking to your content all the time.

6. Pintrest.com (PageRank: 8) – Virtually everyone knows about Pintrest. This is a social media site focusing heavily on photos. So, how do you share your content on Pintrest? Share the photo that you posted as your main image for the content on both the authority site and on your domain. Use relevant hashtags and a solid description to convey just what the image is about. It's not okay to just share the photo. You also have to add a unique description.

7. Tumblr.com (PageRank: 8) – Tumblr, considered the foremost micro-blogging platform, is a great avenue for sharing anything from photos to videos and articles. Again, the use of hashtags is recommended to make your shared links discoverable. But always keep in mind that you should use decorum and tact when sharing those hashtags as well. Don't share irrelevant hashtags. You want to focus and hone them to only 5 or 6

very relevant ones. And ensure that your description is wordy enough but not superfluous. There's certainly a fine art to sharing and not over-sharing.

8. StumbleUpon.com (PageRank: 8) – Quite possibly one of the most popular sites for sharing and stumbling upon content, this should certainly be in your arsenal of tools when building authority and PageRank. Each time you stumble a page, you're adding another high PageRank backlink to your site and building authority over time. Again, do this for all of your links, including both links on your site, and authority site content that you create linking back to your site.

9. Reddit.com (PageRank: 8) - This is a hugely popular site on the Web, where all kinds of content is shared and disseminated. In fact, it's a great resource for taking your content viral if it's the right kind of content. However, on Reddit, you do have to ensure that you're careful that you're not over-sharing. It's easy to get carried away. Find the right sub-board where you can share your content, ensuring that it's useful, and come up with a great descriptive title for it.

10. Myspace.com (PageRank: 8) – This social media site isn't dead. In fact, it still has an insanely popular PageRank and has authority that dates way back before Facebook even came on the scene. Sharing links on MySpace for your content

is a terrific way to generate some authority for content posted both on your site and the authority sites that you post to. Ensure that you use hashtags here again and make sure that your content is relevant to your audience.

STEP #4 – DEVELOP RELATIONSHIPS WITH BLOGGERS

Your next step in building authority has much to do with building relationships on the Web. Yes, this matters, and if you can harness this very important step, then you can propel yourself forward far quicker. So, why is that?

Well, our goal here is to build up authority, correct? So, what better way is there to build up authority, than to get other authorities on the Web to help you increase your own? Now, this is not as simple as it might sound, but does provide a huge leap forward.

Remember, Google's trust is built through authority by getting other people that Google already trusts to link to you. That's why link building is a core component of the work involved with SEO. If you can get those trusted individuals to help you build your authority, then you're one step ahead of the game.

But how does this work? Well, there are several approaches to this. Firstly, I want to point out that this is no easy avenue. You have to drop relevant comments that add to the conversation and spread value before you can even consider approaching authority bloggers.

This takes hard work. I am by no means saying that this will be easy. But, eventually, as you comment and add value to the conversations there, authority bloggers will begin to take notice. Once they've taken notice, you could propose to guest blog for their sites.

What is guest blogging exactly? This means that you essentially write an article that will be posted on their blog. That article will contain one link back to your blog. So, why go through all that work for one link? Well, this is one of the best ways to increase PageRank and authority quickly.

Since Google already trusts the authority blogger's website, a link back to your site, especially if it's coming from relevant content on a niche-specific Website, is huge. This approach should not be discounted whatsoever. Give this a shot and you'll be amazed by the results.

Not only will you increase in Google's overall SERPs, but you'll get the authority blogger's already engaged user-base clicking on your link and checking out your site. If that user-base likes what they see, they might even begin following you.

But, to get to that point is difficult. When you guest blog, it has to be an excellent and well-written article. It has to be error-free and perfect in the grammar department. It must also help to answer a question or fill a need to the best of your ability.

Of course, there's no way that an authority blogger

would even publish subpar posts. So, what does this mean? You have to excel at writing content that not only sounds good, but is also keyword-driven. This is certainly an art in and of itself.

But you know the saying, *practice makes perfect.* You have to practice writing keyword-driven content that doesn't come across as spammy or forced. Get in the habit of trying to write natural and free-flowing prose that goes after your keyword.

We'll get into this in the coming chapters and discuss some of the best practices involved with it. For the time being, keep in mind that you'll be crafting a hefty load of keyword-driven content, so start practicing to perfect your writing skills.

STEP #5 – ENGAGE IN REAL CONVERSATIONS

Beyond the numbers, PageRank and authority occurs one small step at a time, on the people level. Yes, it's important to create high-value content on your domain and on authority sites, share that content, and work with other authorities in your niche to increase your presence.

But it doesn't end there.

Authority is something that extends beyond all of this, and occurs on the micro-level. It happens when you engage in real conversations with people that interact with you on a daily basis. This occurs through blog commenting and social media commenting.

When someone posts a comment to a blog that you wrote, you wouldn't just ignore them, would you? Well, you would be surprised at just how many people do in fact ignore blog comments. They don't engage in real and meaningful conversations.

Think about it this way, would you walk up to someone and start a conversation, then walk away before they answered? Of course you wouldn't. So, why do that in the virtual world. This occurs most often on social media sites like Facebook and Google Plus.

Often, people start conversations on their Facebook Pages by posting something of relevance to their fans and followers. But then they walk away. You have to stick around for a little while to engage your fans and followers and have a real conversation with them.

These are the nuances of building a business in the virtual world, but also the nuances of SEO because they help to build your authority over time. With each conversation, you make a lasting impression as long as that conversation is meaningful.

If you engage in conversations from a perspective of adding value, then you can't fail. Regardless of what the conversation sounds like, if it's sincere, meaningful, and it adds value to people's lives, then it's always a winning scenario.

So, how does this work, really? Well, it's as simple as it sounds. All you have to do is engage in meaningful conversations when it comes to your content. Blog comments, Facebook posts, Twitter posts, and anything else done socially must be followed up with conversations.

But, it doesn't just end there.

To engage in meaningful conversations, you have to also comment on others' posts that are in your niche. Yes, I know that it sounds like a lot of work, and it is. But if you set aside a little bit of time each day, say 30 minutes, you can spend that time engaging in conversations.

People who want to achieve success in SEO often overlook these small steps. It just doesn't happen overnight. No matter what anyone else has told you or what you've read, success in SEO takes time. It takes years to build up a solid reputation and have Google trust you.

But, in the meantime, when you can engage in conversations that are meaningful, people will read those and you'll catch the attention of others. By commenting on others' posts in your niche or industry, little by little, you'll build some traction.

So, get out there and do your best to find a handful of Facebook Pages, Twitter accounts, and blogs that you can continuously engage in conversations on. Ensure that they're popular enough so that others will see your posts.

If your conversations are adding value to the big picture, you'll be surprised by the results you'll produce. Take the time to do this and you'll build authority slowly over time by peaking the interest of others out there that might not have found out about you.

Since the beginning is such a steep and steady climb up that mountain called Google, you have to source other avenues. Think about Google like an IV League College. Schools like Harvard, Yale, and Princeton are hard to get into for a reason.

Similarly, cracking Google's top search results have become increasingly hard. So, you'll want to have every credential that you can to your advantage. And, Google is now taking a hard look at social media activity. Popularity in the social world leads to popularity in Google's world.

4

TRUST THROUGH AGE

Before we dive into an in-depth conversation regarding content creation and some of the best practices when writing SEO-geared content, I wanted to discuss the trust in age component. What does it mean to have trust in age by Google?

If you'll recall back to the beginning of the book, we saw the *Pyramid of Trust*, which had four components. Those components were *Age, Authority, Content,* and *Relevancy*. We've already seen the trust in authority component, so what about age?

Age is an important component in the trust equation, and in order to earn a higher PageRank over time, you have to simply get older. Now, this doesn't mean the age of your domain name. No, it simply means the date from the first time that Google indexed that domain.

So, even if you have a domain name that's 10 years old, if you never did anything with it, and Google never found until say a year ago, you don't really have much age. Now, I would say that this is probably better than a domain you purchased a year ago, but not by much.

So, the importance here lies in Google's ability to find that domain and index it. If it was found a year ago, then it's okay, if it was found and indexed 10 years ago, then you're golden. Of course, we can't all have those kinds of domains.

In fact, most of our domains are brand new. We're usually just starting out with a new site, or we have one that's not very old. So, how are we supposed to approach SEO? What are we supposed to do when we start out with a pre-existing disadvantage?

Well, one thing is clearly apparent here, and that is that Google has drawn a very fine line in the sand. That line is saying that no matter what you have going for you in terms of SEO-related factors, it just can't trust you unless there's some real age to consider.

This means that regardless of how well your pages are optimized for your keyword, or how much authority you've built over the short period that you've been around, if you really want to play with the big boys, then you need age.

When you have age behind you, and the authority that comes along with it, what you'll notice is that almost as soon as you've posted some new content, it will gain significant rank. Like businesses, Google knows that trust is built over time, which is why it gives special weight to this factor.

So, you might be thinking, "Oh great, I have a new domain, so now what?" Well, you have two choices there. The first choice would be to stick it out with the new domain and do the work over time required to build up the rank of your site.

The other option would be to purchase something called an aged domain. What's an aged domain? An aged domain is one that's been around for a while, and for one reason or another, it's expired or the owner has let it go, and it's now available for purchase.

When you understand the importance of a domain that's already been indexed by Google in the past, then you'll understand the importance of having an aged domain. But, if you have an existing Website with an existing business name, this is virtually impossible to make the transition.

You can't just buy a new domain name if your existing domain name is an integral part of your business name. But, that being said, it's still important to understand just what an aged domain name is and how it plays a role in today's search environment.

RESEARCHING DOMAIN AGES

To remove a layer of obscurity from Google's complex search algorithms, let's look at just how to discover a domain's age. A domain's age, as I stated before, has little to do with the date the domain was first registered. The domain's age is indicated by the first time Google indexed it.

With that being said again, let's look at just how to discover Google's historical indexing. For a long time I've discussed using a tool called the Wayback Machine. The Wayback Machine is an Internet Archive that has over 500 billion Website snapshot images indexed.

It's a great tool for discovering the historical content of any domain. It's easy to search and easy to filter through the search results. To use this important resource, simply Google "Wayback Machine" or type in its URL –

archive.org/web.

What you'll notice when you type in your domain name, is a bar graph with results of the site's historical indexing. You can preview any of the captures to get a sense of what your site, or any site for that matter, looked like at the time it was indexed.

This is incredibly useful when you're attempting to purchase an aged domain. Purchase an aged domain? Yes, a simple and effective method exists for doing this. And the best method is to use an auction site through a company like GoDaddy.

Now, let's backtrack a bit. Why would you need an aged domain? You might not want to change domains midstream, but let me argue here in favor for why you might want to do just that. Because, the alternative, with a new domain name that is, will cost you years of time.

Why not purchase a domain name that has already been indexed by Google three or more years ago? It's not difficult and it doesn't cost a lot of money. And, it will save you an immense amount of time. But, there are some restrictions here.

#1 – Historical Indexing Matters

You have to look for domain names that correspond to the niche or industry that you're in. That's because you have to ensure that the historical indexes of that domain are going to match up with the content that you intend to spread.

For example, you don't want to purchase an aged domain about health products if you're running an entertainment blog. That won't work in your favor. This is where the Wayback Machine is so useful. You can actually peruse the pages of the domain that you're intending to purchase at auction before you buy it.

This way, you can ensure that the historical content is going to match the content that you're going after.

#2 – Domain Names that Suffered Google Penalties

Another important point to keep in mind when searching for a domain name at auction, are domains that suffered from Google penalties. A domain name could have been abandoned by its owner due to a drop in traffic that resulted from careless SEO tactics.

So, how are you supposed to tell if a domain suffered from a Google penalty? Well, one important clue comes directly from the Wayback Machine. Is the graph steadily rising or steadily oscillating from high to low, or was there a sudden drop off somewhere?

It could be that the sudden drop off came from a change in ownership, but it could also be due to a number of other factors. So, these are some concerns that you should have. Look at the indexed pages for clues when it comes to this.

There's no absolute way to tell if a domain that you're purchasing at auction has suffered from Google penalties or if it was just abandoned by its owners due to a close in business or a change in their priorities in life. You could research further if you feel so inclined, but be wary.

The point here is that if you see a Wayback Machine bar chart that hasn't steadily climbed over time, then stay away from that domain name.

#3 – Domain Reputation

The last point to note when researching and purchasing aged domains is the domain's reputation. What did the prior owner do with that domain name? Were they running a business, a blog, or some other service? What was the reputation of that domain?

You can run two distinct advanced searches on Google to determine both more information and reputation. You can garner these from Google's advanced "info" search, and "link search. To do this, it's rather simple.

For more information, head to Google and simply type in **[info:domain.com]** using both the brackets and the colon exactly without any spaces. Of course, domain.com would be the domain name of the domain that you're researching.

The info search will give you more information about the web address, similar pages, pages that link to that site, and even cached versions of the site itself. Now, you do have the Wayback Machine for this, but it's great to see what Google has to show for the domain.

The other search is for inbound links to the domain. Since authority and PageRank are what we're after, and the

R.L. ADAMS

quality and number of links essentially equate to PageRank, you'll want to find out who's linking and to what page.

Keep in mind that those links might not all be to the homepage. They might lead to pages on the domain from the past owner that no longer exists. So, those links will be wasted unless you create pages with the same name to salvage those links.

Further, if you do purchase that domain, you could run into link quality issues if you don't hunt down each of those links to non-existent pages on the domain, and update them. So, be prepared to put in the work if you're heading down this route.

To conduct the link search on Google, it's rather similar to the info search. Use **[link:domain.com]** with the brackets, colon, and no spaces. If you add a space anywhere, the search won't work. Again, domain.com in this instance is the domain that you're researching.

94

PURCHASING AN AGED DOMAIN

If you've put some consideration into purchasing an aged domain, or you simply want to see what's out there available for purchase, then the process is rather simple. However, it does differ from purchasing a brand new domain in that ownership isn't granted right away.

When you purchase an aged domain, the process could take anywhere from a few days to a few weeks for ownership to be transferred. It simply depends on a variety of factors from the domain repository, as the transfer process is not as simple as the purchase process.

With that being said, if you're ready to do some research into aged domains, then head over to auctions.godaddy.com, which is simply one of many online repositories where you can search, analyze, and purchase aged domains.

When you arrive at the site, you'll see a search bar somewhere in the middle of the page. In this search bar, you can enter in the keywords for your search to conduct a very quick search. But, I wouldn't recommend doing it that way.

Off to the right, you'll notice an advanced search link. Click that link. Once you do, you'll be presented with a number of options that you can select in order to find the perfect domain. This is important since our criteria for purchasing is going to be specific.

So, what are we looking for exactly here?

#1 – Real Age

We're not just looking for any domain name for sale. We're looking for a domain with real age. What do I mean by real age? I mean that Google must have indexed the site at some time in the past. How long in the past? We want to focus on three or more years.

However, I would suggest initially shooting for 5 or more years. Why is that? Well, this domain will have some authority. Granted, the old pages that could have had links to them might not exist any longer. But, we could still find domains that have a high number of links to the homepage.

How is this determined? Well, we already covered this

strategy using the Wayback Machine. We can analyze any domain of our choosing by using the Wayback Machine, so make sure that you open that site up in a second window or tab as you do your domain-purchasing research.

#2 – Keywords

What are your primary keywords for your site? Are you running a niche site based on a specific topic or section of information? Regardless of what you're doing, you should know your primary keywords. What are they? Have you done your research?

Knowing your keywords, especially when you have a laser-focused site, is important when you're conducting research for an aged domain. We're looking for an aged domain that might possibly contain one of our primary keywords in it.

For example, if we're selling cars, an aged domain with the word "car," "cars," "auto," or "autos" might be the right fit. If we're selling candy, resume writing services, or whatever else it might be, then we also know what keywords we're going after.

Take time right now to brainstorm your keywords. How can you get as specific as possible? This will help you when you select from the advanced set of options available to you when searching for aged domains on sites like GoDaddy Auctions.

#3 – Domain Extensions

Consider the domain extension you want to purchase, but

keep one very important factor in mind. Although domain extensions by country will help you to rank higher for searches done in that geographic location, it won't help to improve your ranking globally.

Focus on purchasing a dot-com domain in the beginning, if possible. These domains will give you the highest overall ranking potential. Of course, if you want to be more specific, you could choose from a number of options today such as dot-co, dot-biz, dot-name, and so on.

In the proceeding image, you'll see the advanced search screen for GoDaddy Auctions. There are just a few things to keep in mind here when conducting your search. If you leave the default settings, then you'll likely come up with no results.

- Keyword: Ensure that you change the default setting of "Exact Match," to "Contains." If you leave it with the default setting of "Exact Match," it will only look for that exact match. For example, if you enter in "cars," then it will only look for the domain name cars.com (or whatever extension you select), and you won't get any results.

- Extensions: Select dot-com or whatever domain extension you're looking for. Or, you could leave this entry blank and get a list of every domain extension available for that particular search.

- Attributes: Select the "Buy Now" option to find domains that are available to purchase immediately and don't require a bidding process.

These domains have expired because their owners didn't renew them for one reason or another.

- <u>Domain Age</u>: This is an important one. Enter "3" in the minimum box, indicating that you're looking for a domain that's at least three years old. You could also enter 5, or any other number here.

Upon conducting your search, you'll get a list of options for available domains. You'll need to trace these options using the research techniques that I already discussed in the prior section. Use the Wayback Machine and Google's advanced search to see the viability of these aged domains.

I would consider this more of an advanced strategy, and it will only give you a small leg up in the race towards developing trust with Google. Your results with this strategy will depend upon when Google initially indexed

5

TRUST THROUGH CONTENT

The importance of good content on the Web cannot be understated. Today, content is king and it reigns supreme across all corners of the Internet. Without good content, you really have no chance in achieving great results when it comes to SEO.

So, what makes good content, well... good? What is it about a specific piece of writing that makes Google want to stand up and take notice? And just how are we supposed to optimize that content for optimal positioning on Google's SERPs?

When we talk about optimizing content, we need to first discuss Latent Semantic Indexing (LSI). LSI is a technology that I discussed earlier in opening sections, but now it's important to ensure that we have a comprehensive understanding of just what it means.

LSI is a mathematical computation that allows us to compare words and phrases in sentences to match up with similar words and phrases in other *relevant* sentences. This gives Google the capability to display similar search results on its SERPs even if the keywords aren't a direct match.

LSI is also a technology that was highlighted during one of Google's recent algorithm adjustments, the Google Hummingbird. In that adjustment, we saw Google entirely replace its old algorithm with the new one in Hummingbird.

So, why did Google call it the Hummingbird? Well, think about the efficiency of a hummingbird for a moment. It can flap its wings up to 80 times per second and can rapidly convert ingested sugars into energy within 30 to 45 minutes.

In a way, Google's shift with Hummingbird was a nod to the efficiency of the new search algorithm, which employs over 200 ranking factors to determine the relevancy of a particular listing during a search. Those ranking factors range from PageRank, to authority, and quality of the content, just to name a few.

We'll get into all the ranking factors later in this book, for now, it's important that we get a good overview of just how Hummingbird works, and why trust in content is the backbone to gaining positioning on Google's coveted first-page SERPs.

So, Hummingbird's importance comes mostly in terms of its efficient LSI-engine, which can accurately serve listings that are highly relevant, even if the keywords don't exactly match. This helps to show Google's desire to move away from exact keyword targeting.

Google's mission to provide the most relevant search results quickly, of course, didn't change with the release of Hummingbird. In fact, it was enhanced. This new artificially intelligent search algorithm has somewhat revolutionized the search engine landscape.

So, what does all of this mean to you?

Well, according to Google, nothing changed in terms of SEOs or optimizing your site. Their aim for you is the same – to produce unique, high-quality content that delivers major value. That's what they want to see. But there's also more to read between the lines here.

Now that search is much more contextual, Google really is going after content that's keyword-centric, but doesn't try to over-optimize for that keyword. For example, you might write an article about "10 Ways to Lose Weight." In the past, you would have optimized that article differently than you would today.

In the past, you would ensure that you met a minimum of 2% exact-match keyword density to your content, amongst other things. Keyword density just means the number of times your keyword appears in your content versus the total number of words.

With that being said, you would have wanted at least 20 keywords for every 1000 words of high-value content. Now, putting 20 iterations of "10 Ways to Lose Weight," exactly like that in an article with 1000 words isn't impossible, but it's hard.

It makes it even harder when you want that content to sound really good. This is where the LSI engine comes into play. Today, you have to take a slightly altered approach. You don't want to repeat the same keyword 20 times.

If you repeat the same keyword 20 times, literally, you might be considered as an over-optimized article. Even if that article provides a high level of value, you'll want to alter your approach. Now, before we get into the specifics of just how to write your content, let's take a further look at this.

LSI, as you now know, is a way to say the same thing with a variation in wording. So, "10 Ways to Lose Weight," can also become "Top Weight Loss Methods," "10 Highly-Effective Diets," or "Best Weight Loss Plans." Of course, we could go on and on with this.

The LSI engine is conducting a comparison of words and phrases, and using it as a substitution. This allows Google to search out the best, most relevant, and most trusted contextual results and display those first, in descending order.

Content is the one area that you'll have the most control over, especially content that's on your site. Of course, authority content is another form of content that you'll have control over, but it won't be total control. There are things you can and cannot do when building out authority content.

Some authority content providers don't allow you to fully control the HTML or CSS elements, or even have a certain number of links in your content. So, content on your domain is the only kind of content you'll have full control of.

But, what you'll find as one of the most difficult tasks in SEO is actually optimizing your content for your keyword. And, taking into account the new search algorithms produced with Hummingbird, you really have to hone your optimization skills here.

Your content has to be keyword-centric but not keyword-stuffed. What do I mean by this? Well, in the past, keyword stuffing was a technique used by Black Hat

SEOs to get Google to artificially increase their rank. They would stuff keywords in the now defunct keyword META tag.

But they would also do things like stuffing keywords with invisible text. Meaning, the text was made the same color as the page so you couldn't actually see it, but search engines like Google would find that text and use it in their ranking algorithms. Not anymore.

Today, your content has to sound good and it has to be optimized just the right way. Now, the 2% minimum keyword density still applies here, but not for the exact keyword itself. You want to have a minimum of 2% keyword density for both your keyword and LSI variations of it.

What do I mean?

Well, here's another example. Let's think about the following situation. We're running a finance blog. On that blog, we post a new article and entitle it, "How to Make Money from Home." Now, how would we find LSI variations of this keyword? And what density would we use?

Let's keep in mind here that we want to have a minimum of 2% keyword density, but not go beyond a 4% keyword density, including our LSI variations. That means we don't want over 40 keywords per 1000 words of content on our site or an authority site.

Now, let's take our keyword, "How to Make Money from Home," and look at just how we would have to structure our content in order to hit that keyword density. Keep in mind, we'll look at the other factors when it comes to content as well. But for now lets concentrate on this factor.

- **30% Exact-Match Keyword** – Given our original keyword at a minimum of 2% keyword density (20 times per 1000 words), and assuming we're writing a 1000-word article, that means the exact match keyword would appear 30% of the time out of those 20 times, or 6 times total.

- **70% LSI-Keyword Match** - Given our original keyword at minimum of 2% keyword density (20 times per 1000 words), and assuming we're writing a 1000-word article, that means the LSI keyword match would appear 70% of the time out of those 20 times, or 14 times total.

Why is this so important? Well, this truly is the heart of your on-page optimization work. On-Page? Yes, On-Page SEO refers to optimization work done on your pages or content, and Off-Page SEO refers to optimization work done away from it, such as through authority linking.

In this section, we're focusing on the On-Page SEO work of constructing excellent, well-written content that provides an exceedingly high amount of value to people. So, with that being said, let's look at LSI variations of our keyword "How to Make Money from Home."

To do that, let's look at the important words here:

1. How

2. Make

3. Money

4. Home

Google's concern is with these four words. So, let's come up with variations for these four words? What are some synonyms for these words? Can you think of them before it's answered here? It doesn't take a significant amount of effort.

1. How

    a. Way(s)

    b. Method(s)

2. Make

    a. Produce

    b. Earn

3. Money

    a. Income

    b. Cash

4. Home

    a. House

    b. Apartment

Looking at it this way, we know that we have to have 14 LSI variations of our keyword. When we look at these, which by the way are only two variations for each of the main words in the phrase, we can come up with a number of different LSI keyword variations.

Keep in mind that you don't need to swap every single word. You can swap just one, two, three, or all four of course. This gives you a number of options to use before you even dive into your content. And, it's best to do this in the beginning to get and stay organized.

1. When you can lay out the keywords required

2. Ways to Produce Income from Your Home

3. How to Earn Extra Income from Your Apartment

4. Best Methods for Earning Money from Home

As you can see, those are just three variations, but the list can go on and on. This is important, not only to have the LSI variations, but to have your content sound good enough to easily flow through these variations. You can create a list in the beginning as a guideline, but you have to ensure that your content sounds natural and organic throughout.

If your content sounds forced or spammy, you can consider it as time wasted, because Google will pay almost zero attention to it. You have to do your research and ensure that you write quality prose that will bring value to people's lives.

Regardless of what you're writing about, content is and always will be king. Anyone that can tell a good story or describe how to do something in the best way will always win out. But why is that? Well, think about the integral role of stories in our lives.

The best storytellers are the ones who are the most successful. And stories are told everywhere in our lives, no matter where we turn. TV commercials tell stories, albeit in a very short timespan; so do movies and sitcoms. Stories are everywhere we turn.

So, the person that can write the best story is always going to win out. And writing content is no different than conveying a story. You want to educate people but also ensure that you don't bore them. Be highly descriptive and use a wide range of words to convey a high reading level.

If it sounds boring or elementary to you, it will be boring and elementary to Google. And believe me, Google knows just how to determine how good or how boring your writing really is. Do the research and convey that information in the best manner possible. I can't stress just how important this really is.

HOW TO CRAFT GOOD CONTENT

Now that you have a fundamental understanding of Google's new algorithm that's evolved through the desire to perfect contextual search and the release of the Hummingbird, let's look at other optimization factors. When it comes to On-Page Optimization, there are several factors to consider.

But before we dive in, let's look at the factors that we're going to consider here:

1. **Quality** – Is the content considered quality content? This is determined by a number of factors that include the degree and variety of word usage, grammar, spelling, and length.

2. **Research** – Is the content considered well researched? Are there statistics and supporting information in there? Are there sources cited? And so on.

3. **Keywords** – Is the article keyword-centric? How often is the primary keyword used? Are there LSI variations of the keyword? Are the keywords used in a naturally sounding and organic fashion?

4. **Engagement** – How engaged are visitors? How long do they stay on the page for? Do they bounce off right away or do they spend a long period reading the content?

5. **Freshness** – How new is the content? When was it written? How valid is the information contained in it still to this day?

So, we have to focus on writing **quality** content that's well **researched**, written from a **keyword** perspective, that's also **engaging** and **fresh**. Sound overwhelming? Well, it doesn't end there. If you hit all five of these factors, then you're doing great, but you could also limit yourself here by over-doing it in other departments.

For example, if a page has a high ad-to-content ratio, even if your content is stellar, but you've overburdened the page with ads, which help to slow the load-time and thus decrease the user-experience, don't expect to rank high on Google's SERPs.

Keep in mind that if you do decide to put advertisements on your site, that's quite okay. But if you decide to heavily weigh down your site with loads of ads, even if your content is good or very good, you simply can't expect to rank high.

Other On-Page Factors

Of course, those factors that affect your content are now clear. But there's still more to the picture. Before we move on, let's look at the other On-Page Optimization factors being considered by Google when ranking content on your Website.

HTML and CSS play a major role in rank. This is both on a page-level and site-level. A variety of factors influence Google's algorithm on a page-level that are important to pay attention to. These HTML and CSS-specific items must be addressed to increase your discoverability.

1. **Page Title** – The page title is one of the most important components of your content. Have you used your keyword or an LSI variation of it in the page's title? This is an absolute must if you want to rank.

2. **META Description** – How well does the META description tag describe what the page is about? Are you trying to stuff keywords or is it a natural and organic description of the content?

3. **Headings** – How well are you using headings in your content? Are you sectioning off your content and utilizing your keywords or LSI variations of it in your content's headings?

4. **Page Structuring** – How much structure does your page have? How easy is it to read? Are you using bullet points and lists? Are your paragraphs too long or just the right length? Are keywords stylized in the content?

5. **Crawlable Pages** – Are the pages on your site easily crawlable? Is it easy to move from one section to the next through a clearly defined menu system? Does an XML sitemap exist? Does an HTML sitemap exist?

6. **Load Time** – Does the page load quickly or does it take a long time? Have you considered any elements that might slow the load time such as any installed objects or components? Are images optimized for Web viewing?

7. **URL Structure** – What type of URL structure does the page use? Is the keyword or LSI variation of it present in the URL of the page? Does the URL use too many server-side variables? How easy is the URL to read?

8. **Mobile Layout** – We talked about Mobilegeddon already. But do you know how your pages look on a mobile browser? Are your pages mobile-friendly? Are the touch elements too close to one another? These are important considerations.

All told, there are many factors involved with on-page optimization. However, this overview should give you a brief understanding. We'll look at Google's specific set of rules for optimization momentarily, but for the time being, ensure that you study and adhere to these SEO factors to on-page optimization.

Writing this type of SEO-centric content that addresses all of the page factors and other site-wide factors when it comes to optimization is no walk in the park. It takes a significant amount of effort, time, and focus to do this and to do it consistently.

Keep in mind that Google isn't looking for just one great article; it's looking for a continuous stream of Massive Value Posts (MVPs). What are MVPs? They're the type of blog and content posts that take 5 to 15+ hours of research and writing.

MVPs involve a tremendous commitment of your time and energy, but are incredibly worthwhile in the end. If you can constantly churn out MVPs, Google will take notice. Of course, you have to ensure that all other factors are addressed, but a focus on MVPs should be a priority.

MVPs can be anything from a large and exhaustive list of resources, to a thorough how-to article. They can take many shapes and forms, but what they have in common is of course that huge value-punch. Don't skimp on that regardless of what you do. You are a representation of the content you distribute. Make it count!

CONTENT RULES

In this section, I wanted to break down the more specific rules for writing excellent SEO content. This will help give you an idea of just what Google wants to see when we create high-quality content that adds value to people's lives.

In the previous section, we talked about how to craft good content. We looked at some overall guidelines when building out that content, but we didn't get into the absolute specific requirements. We saw some quality guidelines along with some technical guidelines.

Namely, the content should be:

1. Quality

2. Well Researched

3. Keyword-Centric

4. Engaging

5. Fresh

In the technical department, we saw that content should:

1. Have a keyword-focused page title

2. Have a keyword-focused META description

3. Use headings to section off content

4. Structure content into lists and easy-to-read layouts

Although this gives you an overview, it doesn't give you the specifics of the rules to follow when you're writing content. So, what are the rules, exactly?

1. <u>Uniqueness</u> – The first and foremost rule is that your content absolutely must be unique. You simply can't write content that's duplicated, no matter what the case may be. If you're quoting sources, then make sure that it's evident you're doing so. If you do copy content and duplicate it, you can kiss your potential for rankings goodbye.

2. <u>Adds Value</u> – Content must add value. No matter what you write, it has to be done from a perspective of sincerely helping others answer a question or fill a need. How much time and

energy you put into it will come across in your writing, and Google has algorithms to determine just how much value it adds. You must convey a high-level of dexterity, skill, and effort in your writing. Don't just slap something together.

3. Well Researched – Do the work to find the statistics and numbers to support whatever claim, argument, or opinion you're making in your content. These make a great supporting claim for whatever you're expounding upon and it will speak volumes about your desire to build inherent trust with Google. There are plenty of resources on the Web for searching out research papers, including even Google's scholar search available at scholar.google.com.

4. Error-Free – What you write must be completely and fully free from all errors. This includes spelling and grammar. Any indication of spelling or grammar errors will decrease the value of your content. When the value of your content declines, so does your potential for ranking on Google's SERPs. Go through your content and check it over two or even three or more times if you have to.

5. Length – Although there's no length that's set in stone for how long your content should be, a general rule of thumb is that you should write content no shorter than 1000 words. Why 1000 words? Well, in order to deliver real value to

people, you have to ensure that you delve into a lengthy discussion on whatever topic it might be. Stick to a high word count but ensure that you stay focused and on the topic, without veering off on tangents.

6. Title – The page title should contain your primary keyword or an LSI variation of it. This is extremely important because your page title is also the title used on Google's SERPs. Pay extra special care to the page title and craft something that draws attention while also utilizing your keyword, within 50-60 characters long. According to Moz.com, if you keep your titles at a maximum of 55 characters, you can expect to have the full title appear around 95% of the time during searches.

7. META Description – The page's META description is also the description that's displayed on Google's SERPs. Ensure that your META description contains the primary keyword or an LSI variation of it. Ensure that the description is also well written and is between 150-160 characters in length, and not greater. If you're using a system like Wordpress to manage your site, ensure that you're able to edit the META description with or without an added plugin installed.

8. Keyword Density – The keyword density relates to the number of times your keyword appears

within your content versus the number of words on the page. So, if your content were 1000 words long, a keyword density of 2% would signify that you should have at least 20 keywords in the text. When you distribute this between exact-match keywords and LSI-matched keywords, you should have approximately 6 exact-match keywords and 14 LSI-matched keywords for every 1000 words of content.

9. Keyword Location – Getting down to the more specifics, when writing your content, ensure that you have your exact-match keyword in at least the first sentence and last sentence. If you can't manage that, then place it at least in the first paragraph and the last paragraph. Why is this important? This drives home the point that this is a keyword-centric article. Not only is density important, but also so is the keyword location. Try not to bunch all the keywords up in one place, as that would also sound forced or spammy. Write natural and organic text with an even distribution of your keywords if possible.

10. Image Quality – One thing you should keep in mind when creating posts for the Web, is image quality. Firstly, ensure that you have the rights to use the image. You can find royalty-free images on sites like Shutterstock.com or iStockPhoto.com, and others. You can also use photos under the Creative Commons License from sites like Flickr.com. Whatever you decide, ensure you can rightfully use that photo, and credit your sources where possible. Secondly, ensure that the photo is

sharp, as pixel-density matters here. In essence, don't use low-resolution or blurry photos.

11. <u>Image Name</u> – Use hyphens to separate the image name using the page's primary keyword or an LSI-variation of it. Further, ensure that you use the image "ALT" attribute to further clarify what that image is about. Google can't read images, so when you're crafting your content, keep in mind that if you want to have a highly-targeted post that's keyword-centric, you have to also focus on the image name and attributes as well. For example, don't use *img71235122.jpg* or something similar to it. Use something descriptive that better describes it, such as *seo-online-marketing-strategies.jpg*, or something to that effect depending on what your article is about.

12. <u>Image Location</u> – Your content's primary image should be located at the top of the page. Whether you need to simply place it at the top or insert it as a featured image will all depend on the theme installed in Wordpress, or whatever system you're using to manage the content on your site. Keep in mind that it's best not to clutter your content with too many images. Keep it simple, select the one best image that fits the content, and place it at the top.

Now, writing unique high-quality content that delivers value is far easier said than done. And, doing it from a keyword-driven perspective is even harder. But practice makes perfect. Get good at this one important task and you will excel at SEO over time.

I've stressed value repeatedly because I sincerely want to drive that point home. I know that you might go out there and read plenty of other material on SEO, but without value, there can be no trust. Remember, trust in content is a core SEO principle, so don't take it for granted.

Practice writing keyword-driven content, both for your site and authority sites, and publish it on a regular basis. Pick a schedule, brainstorm, do the keyword research, and simply write like the wind. You can't get better at something if you don't practice at it.

YOUR CONTENT

I wanted to take a moment to drive home some content points here. Now, we already know that Google is looking for is unique content. I can't help you in that department. If you decide to duplicate content, then you'll be taking two steps back rather than a step forward.

Never duplicate content. Never. I couldn't stress that point enough. Regardless of how lazy or tired you feel, absolutely never duplicate content. By doing this, you're breaking Google's trust. And, why risk ending up in the sandbox? It's just not worth it.

We also saw that content must add value. But what does that mean? Well, you should have a sense of that by now. Considering that you're most likely an expert at searching through Google's search engines, you've surely come across excellent articles and posts in the past.

Although value might sound like something subjective, it's to the contrary. Google has ways of determining the value of content. One way is through engagement. How much time are people spending on that page? Are they sticking around or are they bouncing from the page quickly?

The bounce factor is determined through analytics. Even if you're not using analytics, Google can track time spent by users on sites through a variety of other means, especially when those individuals are already logged into their Google accounts.

Other ways to determine value exist within their algorithms. How many words are being used? Are people sharing that content? Is the author an authority? Are people staying on the site after reading the content and seeking more articles from the author?

Of course, I don't want to rehash everything that I just wrote in the specific rules, but you get the picture, right? Focus on following the rules and ensuring that you deliver excellent content that's checked, re-checked, and even re-re-checked again.

CONTENT-WRITING EXERCISE

This content-writing exercise will be about rich habits. Our goal? Write a 1000-word article that's keyword-centric but not over-optimized. The article title is "Top 5 Rich Habits: Achieving Financial Freedom," and our keyword, as you might have guessed it, is "top 5 rich habits."

That's our exact-match keyword. But can you think of some LSI-matched keyword variations here? There are several that you could come up with. Look at the words "top," "rich" and "habits," closely and come up with some variations for them. How many LSI-matched keyword variations can you think of?

Remember, we want to have roughly a 3-to-7 ratio of exact-match keywords to LSI-matched keywords. But, you could drop that count down to 2-to-8 if you're so inclined. Again, these are only guidelines, and the purpose of those guidelines should be to keep your writing on track for being keyword-centric.

The trick here is not to over-optimize your article. If you can't sound natural and organic, then drop the keyword count so it doesn't come across as forced or spammy. The moment that your content sounds forced or spammy, you could kiss any potential ranking ability goodbye.

The point of this exercise is to help convey just how we disseminate our rules into real and actual content developed for the Web. Reading an article and writing it on your own are two very different things. We learn far more by doing than just by reading or hearing. Action transmutes thought into skill.

So, focus on drafting up a 1000-word article that's keyword-centric around this topic. You could come up with a unique title on your own. I simply used that one to get the juices flowing. You'll most likely need to research rich habits in order to help you complete this article.

While conducting your research, pay close attention to any statistics or sources that might help you with this exercise. How can you incorporate those into your writing? If you're not good at this in the beginning, don't worry. Writing, especially writing keyword-centric content optimized for Google – takes practice.

But, if you're a natural-born writer, then you should have no difficulty in this. Regardless, whether you're good or not, practice, practice, practice. Get out there and start doing research by Googling some popular terms. What are the first listings in the SERPs? What can you learn by reading those?

Find an outlet where you can write this article on the

Web and actually publish it. Setup a Wordpress.com account and create a subdomain. If the subdomain richhabits.wordpress.com is available, then great, if not, find another one.

Keep in mind that this is an experiment in your SEO-writing abilities. Find a great photo that you can use and incorporate it into your article. Rename it top-5-rich-habits.jpg or something similar, and ensure that you use the image ALT tag to add your keyword in there.

Also, keep in mind that, although you can use LSI keywords here, if your image name starts with your keyword, then you have a far greater chance for ranking. Same thing holds true for the title tag and other elements that we'll cover in the 200+ ranking factors of Google in Chapter 9.

R.L. ADAMS

GOOGLE'S WEBMASTER GUIDELINES

Now that you have an understanding about what an ideal piece of content might look like, we have to review the framework that the content should be presented within. That framework has to adhere to the other guidelines in place by Google.

The good news? Google provides this information to anyone who's seeking it out in the form of its <u>Webmaster Guidelines</u>. These guidelines provide a set of rules and best practices that should be used anytime you're optimizing content for search engines like Google.

Now, keep in mind that these are Google's Webmaster Guidelines. These are suggestions that the search giant offers to anyone out there that's looking to optimize their site and their content. This is different than the 200+ Google ranking factors that you'll see in Chapter 9.

What's the difference? Well, the 200+ ranking factors involved in Google's search algorithm are a company semi-secret, not something the company discloses. No one outside of a select small group within Google actually has knowledge of that specific algorithm.

But, what we can do is piece together information from widely held public data, along with information that Google already has personally released to the public, and information based on extensive analysis of things like Google patents, press releases, and employee-distributed knowledge, such as that which comes from Matt Cutts.

Although we've already seen a brief overview of the factors involved, this Google-distributed set of rules and regulations will give you a more complete understanding of just what it takes to rank. This should paint you a bigger picture, so to speak, on just what it takes to ensure that your SEO is done the right way.

Google breaks its guidelines down into three distinct sections:

1. **Design and Content** - These relate to the appearance and layout of the site itself. While these can be considered as aesthetic guidelines, they also have to do with the particular layout of the content itself, giving them a functional purpose as well.

   a. Site hierarchy and text links – From a functional standpoint, Google's aim to provide a rich user-experience has much to do with how easy a site is to navigate. More likely than not, you've had this experience yourself in the past with both sites that were easy to navigate and those that were hard to. Easily navigable sites are critical in Google's eyes because they assist with the efficient dissemination of data by allowing users to quickly move from one section to another without a lot of confusion, and easily find the answers to their questions.

b. Offer a site map to users – A sitemap helps users navigate your site. You'll need both an HTML version and an XML version for Google. Ensure that you have both and that the sitemap is easy to find for users. Usually this means placing it in your footer so that it's visible on all pages. When you design your sitemap, it should allow users to jump from any section to another on your site by clearly structuring your site's pages.

c. Reasonable number of links – From a quality-perspective, Google wants to ensure that your site and content aren't full of dozens of links, especially if those links are irrelevant. It wants a focused number of links, and wants you to keep it small. This is a throwback to a day when link farms would simply churn out subpar content in an effort to create hundreds and hundreds of new links, links that would help those sites be indexed high up on Google's SERPs. Those days are long gone now. Keep the links relevant and to a minimum.

d. Information-rich content – As I've already

stressed a number of times, Google is looking for high-value content. In order to develop high-value content, you have to ensure that your content is rich with information. That information should be well written and well researched of course. So, focus on creating content that strives to deliver this point home.

e. <u>Keyword-driven content</u> – As we've already seen, Google wants to ensure that all content has a particular focus and revolves around a specific keyword. What is the page about? How well is the content targeted towards that specific keyword? Does the content veer off course and go in tangents? The content should be specific, not broad, and tailored towards answering a question or filling some void or need. Try not to get too distracted in your writing and ensure that you laser-focus you prose. Don't try to clutter the page with keywords that simply aren't applicable in an effort to stuff words onto the page or achieve a certain word count. That will not help you.

f. <u>Text links as opposed to images</u> – Images are great for the most part. Except for the fact that Google can't read images. It can't decipher image-based information into textual format. That's where you come in. Today, you can relay many design elements with the usage of CSS and HTML, which will help you keep the graphic-based links on your site to a minimum. Not only will this help to reduce load times, but it will also allow Google to read those links.

g. <u>Usage of "TITLE" and "ALT" attributes</u> – Considering that Google can't read images, it relies on the image attributes to help decipher what that image is about. Of course, it looks at the image name, but that isn't always telling. The next important attribute is the ALT attribute, which provides alternative text about the image. The ALT attribute is the primary place Google looks for information about an image; all image tags should utilize the ALT attribute. You can also use the TITLE attribute to offer additional "advisory information," according to Google's Matt Cutts.

h. <u>Check for broken links</u> – Broken links result in a decrease of the user-experience. Google deems anything that results in a decrease in the user-experience a big no-no and penalties ensue. If you want to save your site from being penalized, ensure that there are no broken links anywhere. You can take this a step further and add a 404-error page that provides links to various different sections of your site. This way, if an incorrect URL is ever reached, Google won't deem this as a decrease in the user experience because you have a 404-error page directing them to the important sections that they might be looking for.

i.   URL rules for dynamic pages – This rule applies to the variables present in dynamic webpages, such as PHP or ASP pages. Google won't index past the first variable, and it's far better to do a non-variable approach to your URLs. For example, you could use the htaccess file to hide your variable-filled URLs and convert those to more semantic URLs that will help to better describe your pages.

j.   Image rules – As you would have already guessed, Google has some rules regarding images on sites that include factors such as quality, dimensions, and location on the page. For example, Google would much rather prefer that you name an image after what that image represents rather than using a name that no one can understand. If the image name is IMG71623523.jpg, that means nothing to Google. Name your images in a manner that helps to best describe them, and use hyphens to separate words. Using your page's primary keywords in the image name is a good habit to get into. If you're writing a post about the "Top 10 Tips for Writing a Better Resume," then name your image "top-10-tips-for-writing-a-better-resume.jpg."

i. <u>Image Quality Rules</u> – Stay away from blurry images or images that simply look unprofessional. Image quality is important to Google. If possible, try to use original images and not images from other sites. If you have to, purchase stock photos from a site like shutterstock.com or istockphoto.com. Or, you can use a site like flickr.com or any other site that employs Creative Commons licensing for its images.

ii. <u>Image Dimensions Rules</u> – Use high-resolution photos rather than low-resolution photos. The dimensions of the photo matters. Keep in mind that screen resolutions are improving at an astounding speed, and regardless of the screen size, the quality of the image is evident to anyone. Stick with large-resolution photos to ensure that you're adhering to Google's user-experience rules.

iii. <u>Image Location Rules</u> – Place the image at the top of the content to convey what the content is about. Don't hide the image at the bottom or clutter the page with too many photos. Be selective with what you present and present the primary photo at the top of the page.

k. <u>Video rules</u> – There are rules when it comes to developing videos for the Web that you can find at schema.org that will make the video more discoverable by Google. The search engine is continuously improving its algorithms for videos, and videos help to make an enormous impact on the PageRank of a given page, especially if that video coincides with the content. Learn all about micro-data and video rules through schema.org if you're engaging in any major video endeavors.

2. **Technical** – Technical guidelines are important to Google's overall rankings. If you want to ensure that your site works and appears flawlessly to the search engine, then be sure that you're following these rules.

a. <u>Reduce or limit the usage of JavaScript, Flash, and DHTML</u> – Today, these technologies have been on the decline, especially with the continuous introduction of new HTML and CSS technologies. You can achieve much of what you could before with the newer technologies, which also help to improve load times and work more seamlessly across browsers and devices.

b. How to handle Session IDs – If your site is using Session IDs to identify visitors, make sure that search engines can still easily crawl the site. This is definitely more of a technical advanced rule, and won't apply to everyone. But, if it does apply to you, and you're using Session IDs on your site, be sure that Google can crawl it just like any real human visitor would.

c. HTTP header support – Ensure that your server has support for the If-Modified-Since HTTP header, because that allows the server to communicate that your content has changed to Google since the last time it visited and crawled the site. This will also ensure that you save bandwidth over time.

d. Usage of robots.txt – Instruct Google and other search engines not to crawl particular URLs or directories on your site with this file.

e. Over using ads – This hits on the user-experience algorithm adjustments that were introduced by Google back during the Panda days. Don't overburden your site with heavy ad usage. Keep the ads to a minimum.

f. <u>Make crawlable pages when using CMS systems</u> – If you're using a CMS system, make sure that the pages are still crawlable by a search engine spider.

g. <u>Cross-browser compatibility</u> – This is a clear and obvious technical requirement. Make sure that your site looks and operates optimally on all major browsers.

h. <u>Optimization of load-times</u> – Google considers page load speeds when determining the rank of a page. Ensure that there aren't any unnecessary elements slowing the load speeds of your pages down. If your page is heavy on the images, consider reducing the number of images used or decreasing their resolution to a respectable figure.

3. **Quality** – These quality guidelines boil down to the specific content and overall practices implemented when you're conducting your SEO efforts. Ensure that you deliver high-quality content and stick to the rules as closely as possible.

a. Basic Principles

    i. <u>Pages designed for users not search engines</u> – Don't try to hide text or engage in other cloaking techniques in an effort to artificially inflate your rank. Design your pages with the value-added approach towards humans, not just towards search engines.

    ii. <u>Avoiding deception</u> – Don't engage in things like sneaky redirects to move traffic from one page to the next, or any other deceptive technique; it's simply not worthwhile.

    iii. <u>Avoiding search-engine-optimization tricks</u> – The word "tricks" can be a subjective word, but try not to employ stealthy techniques to boost your rank. Think about what you're doing and ask yourself if it's coming from a value-added approach.

    iv. <u>Creating unique content that's engaging and adds value</u> – Of course, we've discussed this at length, but this is a specific requirement by Google. Do your best to continuously create fresh, high-quality, unique content that engages and adds value.

b. Specific Practices

i. <u>Avoid automatically generated content</u> – Don't use software systems to generate automated content, whether it's an article, a link, or anything else for that matter. Always curate your content and your links with Google's rules in mind and an approach that's geared towards adding value.

ii. <u>Don't participate in link schemes</u> – Link schemes used to be popular a long time ago, but they can now get you into hot water, even if you pay special care and attention to the style of the link scheme. Simply put, don't engage in anything like this, as it's no longer a viable option.

iii. <u>Don't engage in content cloaking</u> – Cloaking, or hiding your content, is a huge no-no. This includes things along the lines of showing search engines one page while revealing another page to real human visitors.

iv. <u>Don't engage in sneaky redirects</u>
– Again, this is wrong in so many
different ways. Simply put, you
don't want to redirect visitors to
your site to another page for any
reason whatsoever. If they decide
to click on a link to go there
themselves, then that's quite
alright, otherwise, don't do it for
them automatically.

v. Don't hide text or links – Don't
try to hide invisible text hidden
within CSS, or employ some
other means to stuff keywords or
text onto pages that won't be
seen by real human eyes. Again,
ask yourself whether what you're
doing is coming from a value-
added approach.

vi. <u>Don't create doorway pages</u> –
These are similar to sneaky
redirects and exist along the same
lines. Primarily used for
spamdexing, it involves placing
certain keywords to garner traffic,
then using a meta refresh to send
users to a different page.

vii. <u>Don't scrape content</u> – Duplicating or scraping content is the equivalent of self-destruction when it comes to SEO. If you're citing sources, ensure that you're clear that you're doing so. Use quotations, indents, and source names. But don't try to copy or scrape content at all.

viii. <u>Don't participate in affiliate programs without adding a lot of value</u> – Google claims that affiliate links are okay as long as they're limited and that you're clear to people that they're clicking on an affiliate link. But, if your content is thin or spammy, placing affiliate links will only move you further down the relevancy rankings.

ix. <u>Don't add irrelevant keywords</u> – Keep your keywords and tags to a relevant and meaningful number. Absolutely don't try to stuff irrelevant keywords onto a page for the purposes of ranking for multiple keywords. It simply won't work.

x. <u>Don't create pages with malicious behavior (i.e. phishing, Trojans, malware, viruses, etc.)</u> – This is rather self-explanatory, and this behavior could not only get you into hot water with Google, but quite possibly with the authorities.

xi. <u>Don't abuse rich-snippet markup</u> – This might sound like a minor rule, but people will go to great lengths to cut any corner they can find. Rich-snippet markups provide an extra layer of information to Google, but they shouldn't be abused to do things like stuff keywords. Use them wisely and with integrity.

xii. <u>Don't send automated queries to Google</u> – This should be relatively clear by now. Absolutely do not send any type of automated requests or queries to Google.

xiii. <u>Monitor your site for hacking</u> – Hacking is bad all around. When your site gets hacked, it decreases the users experience both aesthetically and functionally.

This could be a change in design by the hackers, theft of credit card data, and so on. Ensure that you're monitoring and securing your site against hackers.

xiv. <u>Prevent and remove user-generated spam from your site</u> – User-generated spam has become too common. Systems like Wordpress have built-in spam modules, but they aren't perfect. Do your best to prevent and remove and all user-generated spam from your site.

6
RELEVANCY

Now that you have a better understanding of the trust components involved with SEO, let's look at relevancy. Relevancy is an integral part of the Pyramid of Trust. Not only is it important to have trust through age, authority, and content, but you also have to have relevancy.

But, what does it mean to have relevancy? The word itself is the basis for Google's business. Its mission is to deliver the most relevant search results in the quickest manner possible. So how is a search result relevant? What differentiates a relevant search result with a less relevant one?

Well, as we've seen already by analyzing Google's SERPs, the competition in some instances can be rather fierce. Two trusted listings that are vying for the number one position can be separated by small factors. How is one more relevant than the other?

To think about relevancy, one can really just think about Google's search algorithm in its entirety. As revealed by Google, the new Hummingbird search algorithm takes into account over 200 different factors to determine relevancy and trust.

Two hundred separate factors are determining whether a particular listing is more relevant than the other. What's more is that Google is performing this function 40,000 times per second, or 3.5 billion times per day.

Every second, computers are comparing over 200 factors, 40,000 times, to serve up the most relevant search results. Just the sheer size and volume of that figure speaks volumes about the amount of work going into search today and the importance that relevancy holds.

Now, we've already seen some of these factors when we looked at the various trust components along with Google's Webmaster Guidelines. However, Google simply doesn't reveal all of the other factors. Nor does it reveal the weight of the factors involved in its algorithm.

Yet, today, we do have a good idea about those other factors involved, even if we don't understand the exact weight given to each of these factors. For example, when it comes to relevancy, things like link diversity and link acceleration also matter.

Link diversity refers to the IP address that inbound links are coming from to your site. The aim? Google wants to see a diverse set of IP addresses linking to your site. It wants to see global authority. It doesn't just want to see all of the links coming from the same sites.

Link acceleration refers to the number of inbound links coming to your site per day or per month. Are the links accelerating from month to month? Are they decelerating? Are you going from 0 links one month to 10,000 links the next?

Google also uses this information to process its Panda and Penguin updates, which are now performing on a more regular schedule. If it deems that you're trying to game the system, your relevancy will drop like a ship's anchor right to the bottom of a digital underwater wasteland.

So, clearly there many considerations to take into account. You have to be weary to try to bend and break the rules. More importantly, you have to focus on quality content if you want to be deemed relevant. Of course, authority is hugely important as well, and so is age.

But, the only thing you're going to have full control over is your content. You can only be deemed relevant if you have excellent content, and you have the other things to back it up. If you're trusted and you work hard to deliver high-value content, you will be deemed relevant.

Simply put, relevancy doesn't come overnight. Both weak and strong relevancy signals come from a variety of factors when it comes to Google's search algorithm. The only way to really push forward and gain relevancy is to ensure that you release quality, unique content that adds value.

Of course, we still need to hit all the other elements involving design, layout, technical, and quality guidelines. In effect, we have to have all of our ducks in a row. But, in the beginning, relevancy will be difficult. When your domain is brand new, it's far harder to be deemed relevant.

That's why our goal at the outset is to go after long-tail keywords. They're far easier to be deemed relevant for. Although the daily search volume will be low, it's far better to rank at the top of a long-tail keyword than to rank nowhere at all for a short-tail keyword.

So, what are some of the ways that we can improve our relevancy? How can we get Google to really trust us and deem us more relevant? Are there ways to quicken this process? Or, are we stifled by the dimension of time?

Well, to answer this question, let's look at the concept of niche Websites. What are Niche Websites and how do they factor into the role of relevancy? How can they help to boost our relevancy in our intended subject matter, topic, or industry?

NICHE WEBSITES

Niche Websites are those that are focused on a single topic or keyword. Any site is considered a niche site if it laser-focuses its attention into one particular area. I'm not talking about a site that has a broad reach and covers a number of topics. I'm talking about highly specific sites.

Why does this matter? Well, when we're talking about relevancy, we have other factors that come into play. Google considers linked content that's also relevant when determining rank listings on SERPs. So, if you have a site laser-focused on habits, your post on habits will more likely show up at the top of Google's SERPs than your competitors.

This is because niche sites are highly targeted towards one topic or area of interest, and any work done through one post, helps to uplift the rankings of the other posts. As more articles and high-value content is added, the more each of the posts, collectively, increases in rank.

Since the posts on niche sites are linked together through the usage of things like keyword clouds, an increase in rank on one post helps to uplift the other. Further, the link juice here gets disseminated throughout the site, because of the interconnectivity of the posts.

Link juice? Yes, link juice is a concept that encompasses the power of a link as it passes through a particular Webpage. If there are no other outbound links from that site to other sites, the link juice stops there. It means that the power of the link increases because it doesn't move away from the domain.

The concept of link juice is an important one to consider, especially when discussing things like relevancy and improving trust. Link juice is the power that a link possesses as it comes into your site. If there are many outbound links on that page, the link juice decreases. If not, it stays high.

Why is this concept important when discussing niche sites and relevancy? Well, in order to increase relevancy, you have to increase your site's link juice. That is, not only does your niche-site content have to be of high value, but the link juice coming into that site must be as well.

Now, this isn't to say that, if you don't have a niche site, you won't be considered relevant by Google. No, you can attain relevancy regardless of the type of site that you have as long as the quality of your content is high. However, niche sites can help you achieve relevancy far quicker.

If you don't have a niche website today, that's okay. As long as you laser-focus your content on a single area of interest such as resumes, habits, personal debt and so on, your site will become a niche site. What you have to learn to do over time is to tailor all of your content towards your niche.

With niche-site content, over time, your relevancy will grow far quicker than if you attempt to do broad-reaching content covering many different topics and not laser-focused on just one. So, in order to build your relevancy, ensure that your content is highly specific and focused.

Although developing a niche site takes a lot of work, so does running any other blog or site. Niche sites are also great ways to rank your content far quicker by using what's called an Exact Match Domain (EMD). However, Google recently did run an EMD adjustment that affected a small portion of those sites.

The EMD adjustment that Google ran affected low-quality EMD sites, those that were registered simply to gain rank and not add value. So, what is an EMD exactly – it's registering a domain with the same keywords that you're trying to rank for.

An example of an EMD would be trying to rank for the keyword search "iPhone 10 Rumors," and purchasing the domain name iPhone10Rumors.com. It could be for any keyword under the sun, as long as the domain name matches the keywords.

There can be extra words in the domain name, but the basic requirements must be that the original keywords are present in the domain. Then, if you develop high-quality content, you have a far quicker chance of ranking that site than with a non-EMD.

This is also the method used by expert Internet Marketers (IMs) to create multiple streams of passive income. By developing several EMDs, these IMs are able to create enormous passive income by targeting low-competition keywords that quickly rank on Google's SERPs.

One perfect example of an individual doing this, and providing transparent data on just what he did and how he did it, is Pat Flynn of SmartPassiveIncome.com. I would highly suggest you check out some of his posts on developing high-quality EMDs to rank for certain keyword searches.

Does this all sound confusing? Well, all of this really isn't that difficult to do. It's not difficult to register an EMD and setup Wordpress in a few minutes. The difficulty is doing the right keyword research and developing high-quality content that will rank and add value to people's lives.

If Google sees you consistently delivering high-quality, unique content, it's most certainly going to give you a prominent presence at the top of its SERPs. The EMDs (or niche sites as we like to call them) are just a way of doing all of that far quicker.

This is why niche sites gain relevancy quickly – they are very specific and targeted to a certain keyword, they are EMDs, and they rank high when they have high-quality, unique content. If nothing else, this should bring to light the importance of laser-focusing your content into one topic.

If you don't have an EMD, that's also okay. This doesn't mean that you can't get out there, register an EMD, and build a niche site. Then, you could create high-value posts that filter through to your original "Money Page," as it's called by IMs.

JUICE TRANSFERAL THEORY

Before we get into a discussion about different SEO strategies and tactics that work today in a Post-Penguin-and-Panda World, let's first discuss the basis of how relevancy is achieved. One important concept to that end is the Juice Transferal Theory (JTT).

Keep in mind that authority largely makes up relevancy. Although it's not the complete picture, to a greater extent, natural and organic links coming from high-value unique content will help your own content appear more relevant.

So, let's look at those how this works? Keep in mind that the basis for ranking on Google's SERPs has almost always been link juice. How much link juice does a site have? In the beginning, when Google was crawling Websites, it did so by going from one link to the next.

The Google spiders of the old days found Websites by

following links from other sites. Then, they took the number of links and ran it through an algorithm, and were able to categorize those links with multiple factors that included PageRank.

Today, of course, there are over 200 factors involved in rank. But, relevancy will still largely be achieved through link juice. How much link juice does your site have? How many organic and natural links are coming from high-value unique content on the Web?

Do you recall our discussion about authority links and just how important those are to your site? Well, relevancy is achieved by ensuring that we build out links coming from other high-quality authority site content and going to high-quality unique content on our sites.

So, the basis of JTT states that the link juice transferred from Link 1 to Link 2 also includes the link juice from all the other links coming into to Link 1. So, if you have Link 1 that links to Link 2, then to your site, you have double the link juice coming from Link 2.

This is because Link 1 is linking to Link 2, which is then linking to your site, so you have this link bridge happening. Why is this important? Again, this comes back to relevancy. The higher the quality of links that are coming to your site, the more relevant you will appear.

JUICE TRANSFERAL THEORY

link 1

link 2

2x link juice

site

Of course, this doesn't mean that you can skimp on content. By no means can you skimp on content. This means that your focus, in order to increase your relevancy, is to collect as many authority links to your content as you can.

Remember the discussion about niche sites? Well, one of the best methods for increasing relevancy is to have relevant niche sites linking to your content through natural, high quality and unique posts. These are also considered editorial posts, because they're from writers with merit.

When writers with merit set out to write a blog post, and then use your article or site as a reference, that editorial content earns you huge kudos from Google. This is the best type of link authority you can garner, and an excellent way to build relevancy.

But how are we supposed to do this? How are we supposed to get out there and get other people to use us as a reference? How can we get other authorities to take notice of us? Well, that's most certainly a great question, and the answer to that is relatively simple.

If you want to build real link juice from editorial content, produced by writers with real merit on the Web, you have to set yourself up as an authority. This doesn't mean you have to have been around for years and years, it just means that your content has to be excellent, well researched, and well written.

Yes, it all comes back to content. But, JTT shows us just how important links to our sites are from other authority sites. If we can set ourselves up as authorities, then we can get out there and start garnering links to our articles and building trust and relevancy in the process.

By no means is this simple. Other ways include commenting and posting on other authority blogs. Why not get out there and write a comment that adds value on another authority site within the same niche or industry as you?

Often, we're so fixated on ourselves that we forget to get out there and contribute to the world. But, that contribution will help to earn you points from other people. This doesn't mean you need to suck up to others. This means that you have to contribute something meaningful to a conversation started by a blog post or article somewhere out there.

This is tough to do in the beginning, especially when we're not used to doing it. But, don't be afraid to take this approach and get out there and contribute to others. Ensure that your name is linked to your blog, and even if it's not, if you post something that adds value, don't be afraid to drop your link into the comment.

OTHER RELEVANCY SIGNALS

So, what about the other relevancy signals involved in Google's search algorithm? We've seen some important factors to this point, but we haven't gone in-depth to truly understand the depth and reach of relevancy signals that are involved in today's highly competitive search.

Well, let's take a step back and see what we've already uncovered. We know that part of the equation is trust. Google can't deem us relevant at all if it doesn't trust us. We've seen how to develop trust in a few key areas, but is that the entire picture?

No, of course not. Google's new Hummingbird algorithm has over 200 factors, which we'll see in Chapter 9. Some of Google's search factors are considered weak relevancy signals, while others are considered as strong relevancy signals.

For example, let's just say you're running a pizza delivery service in Manhattan and someone was searching for best pizza delivery in Long Island, which is outside of Manhattan. Would your pizza delivery shop be a relevant search result for that person's search?

Of course, you wouldn't be deemed relevant. The same thing applies if you're a dry cleaner in Los Angeles and someone from San Diego was searching for "Best Dry Cleaners." If they didn't specify the location, how likely do you think you would come up in Google's search?

All of this is important because it should help to indicate that location is a relevancy signal. This includes both your location and the user's location that's performing the search. How relevant are you to that individual? Sure, you might be trusted with a 10-year old site, but you're not going to appear relevant for those searches.

But relevancy goes even beyond that. The problem here is that there are so many competing factors involved, that to be deemed both trustworthy and relevant you have to ensure that you're hitting each of the boxes and really going that extra mile.

It's not simple at all. Ranking on Google's SERPs by earning trust and being deemed relevant, takes hard work. If anyone told you that there was a magic bullet for SEO, then they're wrong. I say this to make sure that you put in the time and do the work. Stay organized and stay committed.

Since there are so many factors involved in SEO today, you really have to ensure that you do everything aboveboard and truly spend the time on your content and link-building activities. The strong relevancy signals will largely develop from there.

Anytime someone produces excellent content, relevancy is a natural next step. As long as that content is spun and produced the right way, it will naturally earn trust and gain relevancy. It might not happen overnight, especially if the site has a small reach, but it will eventually happen over time.

The biggest factors that will separate the successful SEO from the unsuccessful one are time and commitment to the craft. Yes, you might just be running a blog or a small business, but SEO is now part of what you do. It should run through the very fiber of all that you think and act upon on the Web.

7

SOCIAL MEDIA

We all know the importance that social media plays in our lives today. Most people get all of their news through social media, and conduct all of their interactions on the Web there. Aside from performing searches through Google's search engine, social media activity takes up the bulk of time for Web surfers.

Considering that this is such a cornerstone of our daily lives, focus and attention paid to social media is necessary to succeed in SEO. By ignoring social media, you're ignoring one of the most important tools that will allow you to quickly and effectively reach the widest audience for free.

Now, back in January of 2014, Matt Cutts, the head of Google's Webspam team, stated that Facebook and Twitter weren't taken into consideration for Google's algorithm. Keep in mind that this was 2014. Today, things are a little bit different.

But just to recap, here's what he said:

"Facebook and Twitter pages are treated like any other pages in our web index, so if something occurs on Twitter or occurs on Facebook and we're able to crawl it, then we can return that in our search results. But as far as doing special specific work to sort of say "you have this many followers on Twitter or this many likes on Facebook," to the best of my knowledge we don't currently have any signals like that in our web search ranking algorithms."

When we look at this statement, there are a few things that come to light. First, he stated, "if something occurs on Twitter or occurs on Facebook, and we're able to crawl it, then we can return that in our search results."

What he's saying here is that, if the pages are public, and there was a link share that occurred, then Google can record that link share in its database. Meaning, a share on Facebook or Twitter is counted as a link. Those links help to build authority.

Now, that link shared might not be weighted in the same way as a link shared through other means. For example, a link from great editorial content on an authority site will be far stronger than a random person sharing a link on Facebook. But it still counts for something.

However, something else that Matt Cutts said strikes me as odd. As the head of Google's Webspam team, he has intimate knowledge on the inner workings of Google's algorithms. Why would he say, "to the best of my knowledge," that fans and followers weren't included in the algorithm?

I would reason that today, things are a bit different than they were back then. I would also reason that active fans and followers play a role, albeit a small role, in the overall relevancy of a particular website. The keyword here is active, since anyone can get out there and purchase fans or followers.

Regardless, the important thing to focus on when it comes to social media, are shares. And, what's the best way to get people to share your content? You guessed it. You have to create high quality, unique content that brings value to people's lives.

I keep reiterating this theme of high quality, unique, and valuable content, because it really will be at the basis of all that you do on the Web. You could have everything else done spot on, but if your content is lacking in the quality, uniqueness, and value department, you'll have no chance at relevancy.

Google knows that relevancy comes from trust, and trust comes partly from high quality, unique content, that adds a lot of value to people's lives. That is primarily the basis for their search. Once you've understood that, then you'll turn your focus to churning out excellent content, and not try to skimp in that department.

At the outset of this book, I stated that in order for you to succeed in SEO, you have to do the most amount of work for the least amount of return, initially at least. However, the majority of folks are trying to do the least amount of work for the most return, which seems to be part of the genetic makeup of most of our society.

The unfortunate truth is that you'll get nowhere fast if you try to do the least amount of work for the most return when it comes to SEO. Focus on building very high quality, unique content that adds value to people's lives, and watch how your trust and relevancy explodes over time.

So, when it comes to social media, your focus really should be on sharing the excellent content that you've taken the time to build out. That excellent content will be liked, shared, and re-tweeted, leading to an inevitable increase in authority.

I know that this is a time-consuming approach. Building great content takes hard work. This is not something that's done in a couple of hours, or even in a day. This takes exhaustive research, planning, and repeated execution to get it right.

But, when you do begin to share excellent content, and you're able to connect with people in the social media world, you slowly ease your way into the hearts and minds of the public. If you can do this on a consistent basis, over time, you will gain exposure, and ultimately, you will become an authority.

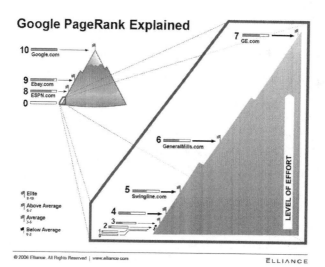

BUILDING A SOCIAL MEDIA PRESENCE

Quite possibly one of the most important ways that you'll connect with people, and get people to like and share your content is through social media. And, building your social media presence should be something that you focus on now, in the beginning.

No matter how long you've been in business, start right away. Why is that? People want to connect with a real person. Gone are the days of B-to-C and B-to-B, and here are the days of P-to-P, or person-to-person. If you're not real, grounded, and able to connect, your success will be fleeting.

So, what are the first steps to building your social media presence? By far, one of the most important tools to do this is to setup a Facebook Page. Whether you're selling services, products, or information, you absolutely must first setup your Facebook page before doing anything else.

Of course, building an online presence on social media goes beyond just having a Facebook Page. But you have to start somewhere. And the place for you to start is on this far-reaching social media site. In effect, you'll have access to billions of people on the planet.

This is truly the next frontier in advertising. As long as you approach your social media activity with grace and decorum, over time, your reach will spread and so will your authority. Facebook is just another way for you to build authority while also connecting with others out there.

So, what are some of the main points to building an online presence through social media? What are the best practices when you're just starting out in order to get traction? How can you grow your page over time and not come across as over-promoting or over-cheerleading?

Well, in order to succeed in social media, you have to employ the same rules that you would employ anywhere else. You have to add value. That sums it up but it's not the entire picture. So, how do we add value in the social media world?

What I normally recommend is to setup what I like to call a content channel. What's a content channel? Well, instead of setting up a social media page dedicated to the name of your business, you should be niche-specific and focus on your content.

What do I mean? Well, I want to use two particular pages as examples when speaking about content channels on social media. One page is called "I Freaking Love Luxury," and it's garnered a large base of fans that actively share, like, and comment on the content.

But, this social media page is more than just a content channel. The content channel simply promotes the lifestyle that's being sold by the company behind it. But, the efforts of the company are rather clever in that they've setup a page not named after the business, but after the lifestyle they're targeting.

You can find this social media page on Facebook at the facebook.com/iflluxury and take a moment to peruse the channel and just how they curate their content to help highlight the lifestyle, but not oversell or over-promote.

This is a rather brilliant move and the channel seems to be growing steadily, and the curated content features high quality photos and descriptions of villas, yachts, private jets, and exotic cars. In turn, they also promote their own services, but not on every post.

Another brilliant social media content channel that you can find is "Inspirational Quotes," available to find on Facebook at the following URL – Facebook.com/InspirationalQuotesHub. Like "I Freaking Love Luxury," this content channel has a similar approach to social media marketing.

The "Inspirational Quotes" page posts inspiring quotes and photos, while promoting their Website and email list on occasion. Of course, these pages didn't get large followings overnight; they had to work at it consistently in order to build out their reach.

Now, say for example that one of these companies, instead of building a content channel, tried to build a Facebook Page just marketing their business. How do you think that would have played out? Certainly not as well as utilizing a popular content channel.

So why is that? This comes back to our discussion

about adding value. People are more interested in high-value unique content as opposed to a business simply trying to sell their products and services. Can you see how this concept of value extends into virtually every corner of life?

I stressed value in the beginning of the book because I wanted to highlight the utter necessity and place it has in life and in business. We all want to get the greatest value for our dollar. Of course, that value can be a perceived value and not just a real value.

But, in order to have perceived value, there must be real value first. What do I mean by perceived value? Well, why does someone spend $3000 on a designer leather bag as opposed to a bag of the same quality at $300 but without the brand name attached to it?

In short, there is perceived value in the brand name product as opposed to the non-brand name product. But perceived value doesn't build up easily – it takes hard work over years and years to do that. In the meantime, you need real value.

Luxury brands didn't become household names by adding small amounts of value. No, luxury brands became luxury brands because of the delivery of real value over time. They built a reputation for always adding huge amounts of value.

So, don't misconstrue perceived value in the beginning with real value. You have to first build up your real value, develop a stellar reputation, and only then can you have perceived value. When we're talking about social media, perceived value comes in the way of large fans and followers to a particular page or person.

Why is that? Well, people will much more likely follow

someone with lots of subscribers because there's perceived value there. But, keep in mind that this only applies to real perceived value. I'm not talking about fake fans and followers. It's easy to find those who've unnaturally inflated their pages with fake fans and followers.

When you build your page on Facebook, you're building your reputation. This will take time. In fact, like your SEO efforts, it will take years and years to do unless you do some serious advertising. But, even then, it will still take a long time to build your user-base.

So, now that we have that understanding out of the way, we would approach our social media presence like we would anything else that we do on the Web: through added-value. Find a way that you can develop a content channel that will add value to people's lives.

Take your given niche, industry, or business, and find a way to develop a channel that's very niche-specific. A niche-specific social media page is what you're going after. Don't be so concerned by naming the page the same name as your business.

By doing that, you might make some traction, but you'll be hard-pressed to develop the same reach as you potentially could through a content channel. What's even better? You could name your content channel after one of your focused keywords.

So, if you're setting up a content channel to help promote your business on a site like Facebook, there are a few things that you should consider:

1. Select a Content Type to Market – When building your content channel, take careful thought about your industry and your business. What do people

want to learn about on a daily basis? This will be the foundation of your social media marketing, so pick wisely!

2. <u>Pick a keyword-rich name</u> – In our two examples of "I Freaking Love Luxury," and "Inspirational Quotes," both content channels have keyword-rich names. But, it's only the latter that has their keyword-rich name also integrated into their URL.

3. <u>Select a Keyword-rich URL</u> – On social media sites like Facebook and Google Plus, you can, in fact, select your URL once you've reached a certain level of trust or fans with them. When you select your URL, try to incorporate your keywords into it.

4. <u>Share Excellent Content that Adds Value</u> – You already know to do this. Come up with some excellent content ideas that are inline with your content channel. How can you add value? What types of things can you share on a consistent basis that people will enjoy? This takes hard work and planning, so be prepared to get your hands dirty.

5. <u>Promote Your Page</u> – In the beginning, you'll have to promote your page. I wouldn't suggest doing this to your friends. On services like Facebook, you could pay just a few dollars per day to advertise your page for fans. Do not buy fake fans. Work on building real, organic fans.

6. <u>Foster Conversations</u> – In social media, it's all about connecting with others. If you take the time to foster conversations with your fans and followers, you'll slowly build your reputation over time. This doesn't have to involve hours of your time. Simply responding and commenting, and stimulating insightful conversations will not take enormous amounts of your time, only an ongoing commitment from you.

7. <u>Find other Niche Social Media Pages</u> – Similarly to the discussion about niche Websites and commenting on their blog posts and articles, you should do the same on sites like Facebook. You can build your online presence by simply sharing your thoughts on posts on other pages. Take the time to show a meaningful interest in what others are doing, and ultimately, it will lead to an expansion of your own fan-base.

8

SEO STRATEGIES

At the outset of this book, we looked at one SEO strategy in particular. Namely, we looked at content marketing. So, why did we discuss that strategy at the outset and not others? Well, by now you should know the answer to that question. Namely, because content is king.

It's also because excellent content is the basis for adding value to the Web. Remember, it's unique content that's well written, well researched, and adds value, which helps to build relevancy and trust. So, naturally, content marketing should be at the heart of any long-term SEO strategy.

But, content marketing can take all sorts of shapes and sizes on the Web, literally. We can market content through online videos, we can do it through podcasts or audiobooks, we can do it through free ebooks, email lists, or of course, through articles and written words.

Content marketing is a powerful strategy because, as we've already seen, it leverages what we call authority sites. Those authority sites will help to give you that added boost that you need to help rank higher, faster. Remember the formula for PageRank?

As you'll recall, PageRank is a mathematical expression for ranking the popularity of a page, or its chances of randomly appearing in search. This is achieved by analyzing the page's authority, or the sum of the number of links to that page and the quality of those links.

When links to your page come from authority sites, whose PageRanks range from 7 to 10, and those links comes from high-quality content, there's virtually no better boost for your ability to show up in Google's SERPs for that particular keyword search.

In the past, I've worked on countless content-marketing campaigns where I spent time, not only writing one core article, but also re-writing that same article 3 or 4 times and posting them to various authority sites. Each one of those authority-site articles contained just one keyword link back to the original non-authority-site article.

Yes, it's a lot of work for just one single and solitary link back, but that's what it takes today to succeed at content marketing. But, as I said, content marketing can take on other shapes and sizes. Video marketing, or even presentation marketing, are two other powerful forms.

What does this involve? Well, one point that I wanted to first drive home is the fact that Google loves high-quality video that helps to deliver value. Similarly to content that achieves those same results, Google will help to serve up high-quality value-driven videos at the top of its SERPs.

What's even better? When you link a high-quality video with a written article, either on an authority site or your personal domain, you help to bridge that PageRank divide. But, this goes back to the concept of link juice and JTT that we discussed earlier.

As you'll recall, in JTT, the power of a link combines the power of other links coming to that page. Now, we're not talking about links to the domain; we're talking about links to a particular Webpage. What's the difference here and how does it affect our strategy?

Okay, think about it this way. PageRank is the rank of importance of a given page on the Web, not of the domain or its other pages itself. So, if we create content on an authority site, although it's an authority domain, the page still has no real rank to speak about.

Still, authority content will always rank higher than content released on your own domain, because, well, it's an authority domain. As I stated earlier, authority domains have an almost implicit level of trust with Google, having been around for ages, and have countless links back to their various pages and sections.

But, you can also supercharge your content marketing. How do we do that? Well, we start creating links back to our authority content, for starters. This happens by sharing the link in social media, but you can take this even one step further.

Imagine this: content marketing your content marketing. Sound confusing? Here's what I mean. In content marketing, you're creating an original piece of content that's posted on your site, correct? Then, you go about creating authority-site content with one single keyword link to your site.

Now, what if we created authority-site content that links back to our other authority-site content? Still confused? Well, the reason why we would do something like this should be apparent. If it's not apparent, I'll use the following image to help depict how this works.

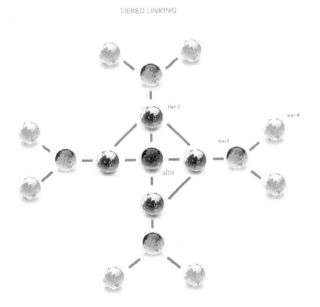

TIERED LINKING

So, what does this image represent? Well, this is what we call tiered-linking. What is tiered linking? This is a more advanced concept in SEO, but I wanted to take a moment to introduce this to you. First, let's carefully analyze this image. What's happening here?

In this image, what you'll notice is that at the center of it, is your site or Webpage on your domain. For the purposes of this conversation, we'll just call it your money page, or MP for short. Your MP is surrounded by other links that are hovering around it, linked in a variety of formats.

This depicts three separate tiers of links that move beyond your domain. In total, there are four tiers, but your MP is at tier 1. Now, by tiers, we simply mean other sites that link back to either your site or to other sites in the tier.

We can also look at this tiered-linking structure like a chain. In effect, this is a link chain, or a series of links laid out in a particular format that has some common elements (link) amongst them. This is an important concept when it comes to more advanced SEO strategies.

Remember, at the outset, I spoke about covering some strategies that will help to boost PageRank faster. Well, this is one of those strategies. But, keep in mind that this is most likely different than any strategies that you might have covered in the past.

Why is it different? Well, much has changed over the years. Google's new algorithm adjustments are looking for over optimization. So, you have to approach your optimization efforts with care and tact. Don't try to throw caution to the wind.

In the beginning of this book, I also introduced you to the different SEO camps for a particular reason. I wanted you to mainly see the difference between Black-Hat SEO and White-Hat SEO, but also illuminate to you that there's a middle ground called Grey-Hat SEO.

Some strategies that are considered Grey-Hat SEO strategies, still work today. They can get you some mileage in the optimization department, but also pose some risks. For example, let's look at one Grey-Hat SEO strategy for argument's sake.

Considering that we've already covered Google

Penguin, this should give you a clear idea of just what's involved today with Grey-Hat SEO. In the proceeding image, you'll see two separate scenarios that are involved with link schemes.

In the first scenario, depicted on the left-hand side, you'll see numerous inbound links that are coming into a site. Now, when I say "numerous" I mean hundreds or even thousands of links that were added either quickly or slowly, but that are inorganic in nature.

For example, hundreds of links coming from PR0 pages or N/A pages in a short period is a clear example to Google that someone is trying to over-optimize. What's more telling is when all of those links are using the same keyword to link to the site.

Scenario one was the primary target for Google's Penguin. In the second scenario, you have numerous inbound links coming into an authority site. In this scenario, there's less risk for a Google penalty. So why is that?

Now, I wouldn't recommend you use this strategy today. There are too many advanced variables involved when doing something like this. However, when you do know what you're doing, there are still some benefits to taking this approach.

So, what's the difference? Well, keep in mind that authority sites already have Google's trust. The reason why a site would get slapped with a Google Penguin penalty is only because of its newness. An authority site is less likely to be slapped with that same penalty simply because it has authority.

Authority is built up over time. And the only way to build authority is to garner trust slowly but surely. That happens by curating quality content, link sharing, editorials, and so on. This just doesn't happen overnight.

So, all things considered, content marketing is absolutely a White-Hat SEO strategy. But, there are twists to content marketing that involve advanced SEO strategies. These still keep you in the White-Hat Camp without stepping over that dreaded line.

Now, these require far greater effort on your part. This is where the content marketing of the content marketing comes into play. If you'll recall, when we discussed JTT, we saw that a link is as powerful as the other inbound links to that page.

But, JTT is enhanced when we're talking about authority sites. Why? Because authority sites already have high link juice, in that many sites are already linking into the domain. Granted, the specific page you create on that authority site might have no PageRank to begin with.

However, when you create some inbound links to that page, you can skyrocket that PageRank in a short period because, again, the domain on an authority site has already earned Google's trust. All you're doing is enhancing the trust of a page on a domain that's already trusted.

This is why authority sites hold the key to your SEO success. This is the only way that you're going to move your site up Google's SERPs in a quick manner without breaking the rules. So, let's take a closer look at the authority content marketing strategy here.

ADVANCED CONTENT MARKETING

I wanted to speak about this advanced content marketing strategy, because, quite possibly, content marketing is going to be your single biggest tool and asset in your SEO arsenal. Once you've mastered this strategy, you'll see your rank swell over time, far quicker than normal.

But, keep in mind that content marketing is no walk in the park. This doesn't bend or break the rules. In fact, it plays precisely by the rules, while leveraging some of the Web's most trusted sites. And the time invested here will pay off in spades.

So, what does advanced content marketing entail?

Well, there are a few methods involved. The first that I wanted to discuss is what I've already mentioned: content marketing your content marketing. Sounds confusing? Well, it's just simple semantics. You're simply writing one authority-site article that links to another authority-site article.

The last authority-site article links to your site, of course. To get a sense how this is done, I've put together the proceeding image. In it, you'll see on the left-hand side, the strategy that we've already discussed, simple content marketing.

In simple content marketing, you're creating one piece of content marketing on an authority site to market a single piece of similar content on your site. This can be done multiple times over. The more pieces of content created on authority sites linking back to the MP, the higher its link-juice becomes.

But it's the second strategy, which we see on the right-hand side of the image, that's far more powerful. You're also creating that authority-site content (first tier) that's similar to the content on your site or MP, then going out there and creating additional authority-site content (second tier) that links back to the first tier of authority-site content.

The reason why this is a powerful approach comes back to the issue of trust and relevancy. Since authority sites already have implicit trust with Google, it's far easier to increase the PageRank of an authority-site page than a page on your domain that might be lacking authority.

How does this differ from sending massive links into the authority sites like we saw in the previous example in the last section? Well, with that you run the risk of a penalty. But, these aren't just any links; these are authority-site content links.

The point here is that you're writing high-quality, unique authority-site content that adds value to people's lives. This isn't just about creating hundreds or thousands of inbound links. But we can go even one step further in our strategy here.

Again, I'll remind you that PageRank is derived from the total sum and quality of the inbound links to a page. We can easily increase authority-site PageRank as opposed to PageRank on our domains. So, we can engage in even more advanced strategies to do just that.

In the preceding image now you'll see a third strategy. This link chain is far more powerful when done right. Again, I want to remind you that this can't be done based on low-quality content. To the contrary, you must use extremely high-quality content here.

So, in the third strategy, we have two tiers of authority-site content again. But, unlike in the second strategy, our second tier is a single authority site as opposed to multiple authority sites. That single authority site on the second tier also gets multiple social media shares into it.

But, why go to all of this trouble? Why do things have to be so difficult? Again, today, you're facing multiple obstacles when it comes to SEO. You have the algorithm hurdles that you need to cross from Google, but you also inherent trust and relevancy issues to deal with on your site.

Sure, you could be doing everything else perfectly, but without inherent trust and relevancy, which is only developed over time, you could kiss your potential for rankings goodbye unless you focus and concentrate your efforts on authority-site content marketing strategies.

As you implement these strategies, pay careful attention to the PageRank of the pages that you're optimizing. For example, after you build your first tier of authority site content, begin tracking the PageRank of your MP and that first tier.

Use a spreadsheet and jot down the PageRank to your first tier and MP daily or weekly. Then, after you build your second tier, add that tier onto your spreadsheet. As you add the social media links and other links, track your PageRank to all pages as you steadily go ahead.

You have to get organized so you can see what's

working here for you and what isn't over time. Remember, SEO isn't an overnight process. Real SEO takes hard work exerted over the long term. It involves constantly churning out high-quality content that brings value to people's lives.

So, ensure that you're using whatever means are available to you in order to track and analyze your results. How are you improving from week to week? How are you improving from month to month? Don't get discouraged in the beginning if you don't see enormous improvements. It will take time.

But, focusing on authority-site content is going to pay off enormously for you as long as you spend the time with this. Don't try to outsource this in the beginning. You'll find it extremely expensive to find quality SEO writers.

As an SEO specialist, you're in the marketing business. You're expected to know how to market, and that involves curating content and analyzing your results to see what works and what doesn't. So, try to excel at each of the areas personally before you even consider finding outside help.

9

200+ GOOGLE RANKING FACTORS

Now that you have a rather comprehensive understanding of SEO, let's look at Google's algorithm and all the ranking factors involved. As you may now know, Google's newly revamped Hummingbird search is now using over 200 factors to determine rank.

Throughout the course of this book, we've looked at many of those factors, but what are the rest? Well, let's break them down here. But, before I do, I want to issue a disclaimer that some of these factors are documented, some are disputed, and some are speculated based on data.

This is not hard scientific fact, but it's as close to the truth as we can possibly get. Keep in mind that things are also changing rather quickly in today's search engine environment. But it also seems as though things are beginning to level out.

Something that we do know is that Google will continue to focus its efforts on mobile rather than desktop. Google has informed us that mobile searches have now surpassed desktop searches for the first time in 10 countries that include both the US and Japan.

This is significant, and Google's Mobilegeddon algorithm adjustment should give you a clear indication of just where things are heading. If you're not designing your site and content for mobile and other devices, then you could be left behind in the digital dust.

But, how are these ranking factors different from Google's Webmaster Guidelines? Don't those provide the information needed from Google to optimize our sites? Well, yes, but they don't paint the full and complete picture. Why not?

Well, Google doesn't want to reveal their exact algorithm and just how much weight is given to each ranking factor. If it did, it would have a continued abuse of the system. What Google has done is to set this game called the Web up for grabs by making it a trust and relevancy race.

As you know, trust and relevancy are the primary building blocks to Google's ranking system. And in order to get Google to trust you and deem you relevant, you have to deliver an exceedingly high level of value in all shapes and forms. If you can achieve those things, then you're winning.

All of the ranking factors that Google has in place create a framework for analyzing and determining that trust and relevancy. How trustworthy and relevant are you in the eyes of Google? This comprehensive checklist is a great way to help guide your work and your efforts.

The following list will also help to illuminate some things that might not have been clear to you before. Now, all of these are derived from existing Google patents, information released by the company itself, or relevant data and statistics gathered throughout the Web.

This list is not perfect and it's not exact. But it's most likely the closest that we could come to determining the ranking factors and their importance in Google's present search algorithms.

So, what are the 200+ ranking factors that are included in Google's new algorithm? Well, as you would already guess, these are split into two categories:

1. <u>On-Page Optimization</u> – Everything that happens with SEO on the page itself. When speaking about content on your domain, we're talking about all Website-related factors.

2. <u>Off-Page Optimization</u> – Everything that happens with SEO off the page. Here, we're talking about things like link-building, social media, content marketing, domain data, and so on.

Of the two categories, we have far more control over what happens on the page, and far less control over what happens off the page. That doesn't mean that we can't influence the off-page factors, it just means we have far less sway over them.

For example, when speaking about links generated, editorial content, reviews left, or any other off-page factor, we can influence these, but at the end of the day, since they're happening away from the page that we have control over, we can't command what actually happens there.

Of the two categories, there are seven separate sub-categories when it comes to the 200+ ranking factors that go into Google's algorithm. The full list goes as follows:

1. On-Page Optimization

   a. Content Factor

      i. **Quality**

         1. <u>Word range usage or page reading level?</u> – Is the content at a high reading level or does it use elementary words with a low range.

         2. <u>Page & image load speed?</u> – How quickly or slow is the page loading? If the page loads slowly, that decreases the user experience, thus decreasing rankings.

         3. <u>Keyword density?</u> – What is the keyword density of the page? How many times are the keywords used in relation to all the other words in the content? Is

it clear that the page is about this particular keyword? Does it seem over-optimized or is it just perfect?

4. <u>LSI keyword density?</u> – What's the LSI keyword density? Does the LSI keyword density help to reinforce the page's primary keyword? Do the LSI keywords seem natural and organic in the overall flow of the text?

5. <u>Stylized keywords?</u> – Have keywords been stylized in bold, italics, or underline font? This could be a weak relevancy signal.

6. <u>Stylized LSI keywords?</u> – Have the LSI keywords been stylized in bold, italics, or underline font? This too could be a weak relevancy signal.

7. <u>Keyword or LSI keyword in first paragraph?</u> – Does the keyword or LSI keyword appear once in at least in the first paragraph or first 100 words?

8. <u>Keyword or LSI keyword in last paragraph?</u> - Does the keyword or LSI keyword appear once in at least the last paragraph or last 100 words?

9. <u>Duplicate content?</u> – Has the content been duplicated from another source?

10. <u>Image optimization?</u> – Are images optimized? Are descriptive image names being used? Is the image a high-resolution photo?

11. <u>Image ALT tag keywords present?</u> – Is an ALT tag being used

to describe with the page's primary keyword?

12. <u>Image name keywords present?</u> – Is the primary keyword present in the image name?

13. <u>Number of outbound links?</u> – How many outbound links away from the content exist on the page? Too many outbound links may decrease the quality of the content.

14. <u>Quality of outbound links?</u> – Are the outbound links high-quality links that are relevant to the content on the page? Are the outbound links linking out to authority sites?

15. <u>Theme of outbound links?</u> – Do the themes of the outbound links match the theme of the page? Google could be

using the outbound link page's theme as a relevancy signal.

16. <u>Grammar and spelling?</u> – Does the page use proper grammar and spelling? Although a weak relevancy signal, excessive grammar and spelling errors could indicate low-quality content.

17. <u>Syndicated content?</u> – Is the content on the page original or was it copied from another source? If it was copied, was it sourced? Syndicated content won't rank as high as original, unique content.

18. <u>Audio & video on page?</u> – Relevancy signals indicate that high-quality audio, video, or other multimedia on the page increases the quality of the content.

19. <u>Number of internal links to page on site?</u> – Signifying the importance of a page on a particular site, multiple internal links to the same page can be an increased relevancy signal.

20. <u>Quality of internal links to page on site?</u> – Pages on your site with high PageRank and other positive relevancy signals have a greater impact linking to any other particular page on your site.

21. <u>Number of outbound links in your content?</u> How many outbound links are present in the content? Are these nofollow links or dofollow links? Although nofollow links are better in terms of SEO, too many nofollow links might also signify excessive link curating.

22. <u>Internal link anchor text?</u> – Are there internal links in your content pointing to other content on your site? What anchor text is being used? Although this is a relevancy signal, it's relatively weak, but still one that Google uses to understand the bigger picture of your content.

23. <u>Internal link title attribution?</u> – Do you have title tags in your internal links on your content? If so, what keywords are being used in them? Are they reinforcing the content's primary keyword or pointing to a secondary page that helps to reinforce the existing content?

24. <u>Broken links on page?</u> – An excessive number of broken links can indicate that a site has either been abandoned or put together carelessly. Broken links also decrease the user's

experience. And, anything that decreases the user's experience, decreases relevancy.

25. Affiliate links present? – Are affiliate links present? Google doesn't like affiliate links, but will tolerate them as long as they're not excessive and your policies do indicate that some of your links will generate you an income if they purchase from them.

26. Hidden affiliate links? – Quite possibly one of the worst things that you can do. If you're hiding your affiliate links, then you're cloaking your content. And, by now, you should know that this is absolutely not tolerated by Google. Expect a drop in rank if you do this.

27. PageRank? – What's the PageRank of the page?

Has the page built some authority? Pages with a higher PageRank will have a greater chance of appearing randomly in Google's SERPs if all other factors are equal.

28. <u>Host domain PageRank?</u> – What's the PageRank of the host domain? This is a moderate relevancy signal. Remember the importance of PageRank to authority sites? If the host domain has a high PageRank, this will help the underlying content on any page of that site.

29. <u>Age of the page?</u> – How old is the page? When was it first published? Freshness counts for some topics, but Google also looks to content's overall age as a relevancy signal.

30. <u>YouTube video?</u> – Does the page include a YouTube video?

Multimedia on the page, especially videos that reinforce the content, is a moderate relevancy signal to Google.

31. <u>Linking to bad link neighborhoods?</u> – Do you have links going out to bad link neighborhoods? This could be a weak relevancy signal and an indication of low-quality content.

32. <u>Over optimized page content?</u> – Have you gone overboard with optimizing for your keyword? Is your keyword density too high, making the content sound unnatural or forced? This will result in a small penalty.

33. <u>Auto-generated content?</u> – Have you auto-generated your content with a software system to spin or re-rewrite

something that resulted in poor quality content? Stay away from these frowned-upon practices.

ii. Research

1. <u>Research sources cited?</u> – Have you cited sources or Websites with information from research studies or other quotes and references that you've provided?

2. <u>Statistical information provided?</u> – Have you provided statistics and figures to backup any claims that you've made in your writing?

iii. Length

1. <u>Is the content over 1000 words in length?</u> – Content over 1000 words will rank higher than shorter content.

2. <u>Is the content over 2000</u>

words in length? —
Content over 2000
words but under 2500
words generally tends to
rank the highest on
Google's SERPs.

iv. Engagement

1. Time spent on page? —
   How much time are
   visitors spending reading
   your page? How engaged
   are they?

2. Bounce rate? — What
   percentage of visitors
   leaves after visiting your
   page from Google's
   SERPs? High bounce
   rate could indicate that
   the visitor's question was
   answered as long as the
   visitor spent enough
   time reading your
   content.

3. Exit rate? — Are visitors
   moving to other pages
   on your site after
   visiting? If so, what
   other pages, and what
   are the exit rates from

those pages?

v. Freshness

1. <u>Recent content or updated content?</u> – How fresh is the content? We know that age matters, and that older content generally tends to rank higher than newer content. However, older content could and should be updated with new information when and if it becomes available.

2. <u>Magnitude of content updates?</u> – If content was recently updated, what's the magnitude of the update? Was it just a few words changed here and there or did sections and entire pages get overhauls?

3. <u>Historical updates to page?</u> – What are the historical updates to the page? How many times has the page been

updated and what types of updates occurred?

vi. Thinness

1. <u>Low word count?</u> – Thinness is a penalty. If you keep your content's word count very low, you can expect to rank low or nowhere at all on Google's SERPs. If the content is thin, consider adding a YouTube video to help boost the quality and counteract the thinness. But, overall, you should consider always keeping your word count above 1000 words.

2. <u>Low quality?</u> – What's the reading level of the content? Is the quality low? Was this just thrown together quickly, or was it well written and well thought out?

vii. Number of Ads

1. <u>Ads above the fold?</u> –

How many ads exist above the Website's fold? Does this decrease the user's experience?

2. <u>Ads below the fold?</u> – How many ads exist below the fold and where do they exist? Do the ads disrupt the user's experience?

b. HTML & CSS Factor

i. **Page Title**

1. <u>Keywords in title?</u> – Are the primary keywords used in the page's title?

2. <u>Keywords starting title?</u> – Do the primary keywords start the title of the page? This is a strong relevancy signal.

3. <u>LSI keywords in title?</u> – Are LSI keywords used in the page title?

4. <u>LSI keywords starting title?</u> – Do the LSI keywords start the page's title?

ii. META Description

1. <u>Keywords in META description?</u> – Does your primary keyword exist in the META description? This is a moderate relevancy signal.

2. <u>Keywords starting META description?</u> – This is a weak relevancy signal, but also might be a sign of over-optimization.

3. <u>LSI keywords in META description?</u> Do LSI keywords exist in the META description? This is a moderate relevancy signal.

4. <u>LSI keywords staring the META description?</u> Another relevancy signal,

but could be stronger than the primary keyword starting the META description, since it looks more organic in nature.

5. Spammy META tag? – Do you have a spammy, keyword-stuffed META description? Is it difficult to read?

iii. Page Headers

1. Keywords in H1 tag? – Is the page's primary keyword in the H1 tag? In some systems like Wordpress, the H1 tag is also used as the title of the page.

2. Keywords starting H1 tag? – Do the keywords start the H1 tag? This is a moderate to strong relevancy signal.

3. LSI keywords in H1 tag? – Do the LSI keywords

exist in the H1 tag?

4. <u>Keywords in H2 or H3 tags?</u> – Does the primary keyword exist in the H2 or H3 tags?

5. <u>Keywords starting H2 or H3 tags?</u> – Does the primary keyword start the H2 or H3 tags? This might be good, but it also might be a sign of over-optimization. Be wary when implementing this.

6. <u>LSI keywords in H2 or H3 tags?</u> – Do the LSI keywords exist in the H2 or H3 tags? This could be a positive relevancy signal as it moves away from over-optimization.

7. <u>LSI keywords starting H2 or H3 tags?</u> – Do the LSI keywords start the H2 or H3 tags? Another positive relevancy signal as it also moves away

from over-optimization.

iv. Page Structure

1. <u>Layout quality?</u> – Is the overall page easy to read and follow? How about the navigation? Can you easily move from one section of the site to another?

2. <u>Sectioned and easily readable content?</u> – Has the page been broken down into sections with easily readable content?

3. <u>Usage of lists and bullet points?</u> – Are lists being used with bullet points or numbers? This is a moderate relevancy signal.

4. <u>Wordpress tags?</u> – Are Wordpress tags being used? This is a weak relevancy signal and only

allows relating one page or a group of pages to others.

5. <u>Priority of page in sitemap?</u> – How high up is the page in the sitemap hierarchy?

v. Keyword Stuffing

1. <u>Over usage of keywords?</u> – Have you overused your keywords? This could result in a moderate to severe Google penalty.

vi. Hidden Text

1. <u>Invisible text with CSS?</u> – Have you hidden text anywhere on the page using CSS? This could result in a penalty.

2. <u>Text placed a far distance below page end?</u> – Have you tried to hide text by placing it far away from the page's

visible elements, such as far off down the page past where the visitor would generally stop reading? This could result in a penalty.

c. Website Architecture

  i. **Website & Crawlability**

  1. <u>Number of pages?</u> – How many pages exist on the site? Are they properly organized and easily reachable from any other page on the site?

  2. <u>Sitemap present?</u> – Is an HTML and XML sitemap present?

  3. <u>Site uptime?</u> – Does the site suffer from elongated down times or have other hosting problems that could have an effect on the user's experience?

  4. <u>SSL certificate?</u> – Is this

a secure site using SSL encryption with a certificate from a trusted provider? SSL sites will rank higher in Google's SERPs.

5. <u>Terms of service & privacy pages?</u> – Do you have terms of service and privacy pages on your Website? This could be a weak relevancy signal.

6. <u>Breadcrumb navigation?</u> – Another weak relevancy signal to move through a stack of related pages.

7. <u>Easy to navigate?</u> – Overall, is the site easy to navigate? Can we move from one section to the other without much difficulty?

8. <u>Usage of Google Analytics?</u> – Although not documented, many

believe that the usage of Google Analytics is a weak relevancy signal.

9. Usage of Google Webmaster Tools? – Although not documented, many believe that the usage of Google Webmaster Tools is a weak relevancy signal.

ii. Duplicate Content

1. Duplicate text throughout site? – Do your pages have repetitive text in them? Are you repeating certain paragraphs, sentences, or keywords in the same manner on your pages? This could result in a decrease in relevancy.

2. Duplicate META content? – Do you have duplicate META content on your pages? Are you using the same META description on multiple pages? This could result

in a decrease in relevancy.

iii. Site Speed

1. HTML load time? – How quickly does the HTML load on your page? Slow pages will decrease the user experience.

2. Google Chrome load speed? – How quickly does your site load in Google Chrome?

iv. Page URLs

1. Canonical URL? – Are you using canonical URLs that are easy to read and understand, and accurately depict the content of the page?

2. Keyword in URL? – Is your page's primary keyword present in the URL?

3. <u>Keyword at start of URL?</u> – Does your page's primary keyword start the URL? This could be a moderate to strong relevancy signal.

4. <u>LSI keyword in URL?</u> – Are LSI keywords present in the page's URL?

5. <u>LSI keyword start of URL?</u> – Does your URL begin with one of your LSI keywords?

6. <u>URL length?</u> – Is your URL too long, or just the right length? Stay from very elongated URLs and from stuffing keywords unnaturally in them.

7. <u>URL path?</u> – Does the URL path help to reinforce the relevancy of the page?

8. <u>URL string?</u> – Is there a URL string that's incorporating too many variables? Google won't read beyond the first variable in a URL string after the question mark for example.

v. Mobile-Friendlines

1. <u>Is site mobile friendly?</u> – Is your site mobile friendly? Can visitors easily navigate and read the site on a mobile browser or do the elements get confusing?

2. <u>Is site mobile optimized?</u> – Are the touch elements too close to one another? Is the page optimized for mobile?

2. Off-Page Optimization

    a. Links

i. **Link Quality**

1. <u>Domain age</u> – How old is the domain that's linking to you? This is a strong relevancy signal as it's also an underlying factor in authority. Older domains will have built more authority over time.

2. <u>IP diversification</u> – How diverse are the IP addresses for the links coming to your site? Keeping all your links to only a group of IP addresses doesn't indicate authority. Google wants to see global authority.

3. <u>Link text</u> – What words are being used in the link text? Does the link seem natural and organic? Or, does it seem like the same link text is being used repeatedly?

4. <u>Keyword in link text?</u> – Is the page keyword

213

being used in the off-
page link text? This is a
relevancy signal, but it
can be abused.

5.   <u>LSI keyword in link text?</u>
     – Is the LSI keyword
     being used in the link?
     This could indicate
     higher relevancy when
     coming from the right
     type of content,
     comment, or post.

6.   <u>.EDU links? .GOV
     links?</u> – Depending upon
     the PageRank and
     content of these links,
     it's a widely held notion
     that they deliver more
     link juice.

7.   <u>Linking page authority?</u>
     – How much authority
     has the linking page
     built? Keep in mind, this
     isn't the authority of the
     domain, but the page
     where the link is coming
     from. A link from a page
     with more authority will
     be an increased relevancy

signal.

8. <u>Linking page relevancy?</u>
— How relevant is the linking page to your page? Does the content there have some tie-in to the content on your page? This is another moderate relevancy signal.

9. <u>Word count on linking page?</u> — How many words are there on the page containing the content that's linking to you? Is the link coming from within that content or from a sidebar or footer?

10. <u>Quality of linking content?</u> — Remember, high quality content that links back to your high quality content is a great relevancy signal.

11. <u>Linking domain relevancy?</u> — How much

relevancy does the top-level domain on the linking page have to your content?

12. Liking domain authority? – How much authority does the top-level domain have? How many links are there going to the domain? SEO Quake sheds some light on this for us as we've already seen.

13. Links from competitors? – Do you have links from competitors? This could be a relevancy signal.

14. Social shares of referring links? – How many people have shared the link of the page that's linking to your content?

15. Guest post link? – Guest posts are a good relevancy indication, especially when the guest

post comes from a relevant site with some authority, but not as good as positive editorial content.

16. Bad link neighborhood? – Do the links come from a neighborhood filled with bad links? For example, link farms or any other site that might have been given a Google penalty might negatively affect your relevancy.

17. Nofollow or Dofollow link? – Google doesn't follow "nofollow" links. Matt Cutts once stated, "In general, we don't follow them." Try to get links without this attribute, or the "dofollow" attribute for increased relevancy.

18. Link type diversity? – Is there diversity in this link from previous links? Are all the links coming from

the same place or do
they have some
diversity? Google likes to
see a wide range of sites
linking in and not just
the same sites over and
over again.

19. <u>Sponsored link?</u> – Links
coming from sponsored
content won't have as
much link juice as those
coming from natural,
organic, or editorial
content.

20. <u>Contextual link?</u> – Do
the links come from
empty pages or profile
pages with no other
data? These could reduce
the relevancy signal and
link juice of those links.

21. <u>Excessive 301 redirects?</u>
– Has the linking page
moved from another
domain or URL? If there
are excessive 301
redirects from the
linking page, this could
be a decreased relevancy

218

signal.

22. <u>Anchor text of link?</u> – How natural is the anchor text in the link? Is it placed organically within content or does it seem forced, spammy, or unnatural?

23. <u>Title tag of link?</u> – Is the link using a title tag to help reinforce the relevancy of it? Title tags in links are similar to the ALT tags used in images.

24. <u>Location of link on page? Footer, sidebar or within page content?</u> – Footer and sidebar links have less relevancy than links placed organically within content.

25. <u>Link comes from a poor review or a recommendation?</u> – Google can determine whether the link is coming from negative

content or positive content about the page being linked to.

26. <u>Links from top resource pages?</u> – Top resource pages on the Web are links that have enormous authority and generally come from elongated list posts.

27. <u>Link from authority site?</u> – Is the link coming from an authority site domain?

28. <u>Wikipedia links?</u> – Is the link coming from Wikipedia? Wikipedia is a site with an enormous level of trust built with Google, and links from them hold more relevancy and carry much more link juice than standard links.

29. <u>Link age?</u> – How old is the link? How long has the link been around for?

The older the link, the more relevancy it tends to extend.

30. <u>Links from real sites?</u> – Is the link coming from a site with little traffic that was just setup in an attempt to build more links? Or, is the link coming from a real site with real traffic and user interaction? Google can differentiate between the two.

31. <u>Natural link?</u> – Is the link a natural and organic link, or is it some form of paid or advertised link? Is it coming from natural and organic content?

32. <u>Reciprocal link?</u> – Is this just a reciprocal link? These hold less relevancy. For example, if you were to exchange links with someone, it won't hold as much importance as a natural

link.

33. Links from 301 page? –
Are the links coming
from a page that's
recently moved to a new
URL or domain? These
could have decreased
relevancy.

ii. Link Number

1. Separate referring root
domains? – How many
links are coming from
different domains?

2. Excessive low quality
links? – Too many low
quality links from low
PageRank or spoof pages
will decrease your
relevancy.

iii. Link Velocity

1. Positive link velocity? –
Are the number of links
increasing from month
to month?

2. <u>Negative link velocity?</u> – Are the number of links decreasing from month to month?

3. <u>Unnatural link velocity?</u> – Are there too many links coming in? For example, did the site go from 100 links to 10,000 links in one month? This is partly the basis for the Google Penguin penalty.

iv. **Paid Links**

1. <u>Excessive paid links?</u> – Is the site purchasing links, and doing so excessively? Is there a high ratio of paid to natural links happening?

v. **Spammy Links**

1. <u>Spammy link text?</u> – Is the link within the text spammy or unnatural? Is the link coming from a page with no content in an effort to simply build

223

relevancy?

2. Poor quality links? – Are the links poor quality? Do they come from real content or empty pages? Do the pages contain spammy text?

b. Trust Factors

i. **Content**

1. Useful content? – How useful is the content that's linking to your page?

2. Content provides value? – How much value does the content provide that's linking to your page?

3. Content provides unique insights? – Does the content linking to you provide unique insights?

4. Contact us page? – Is

there a contact us page present with information? Google uses this to determine real sites from fake sites.

ii. Authority

1. <u>Link selling?</u> – Is the page that's linking to you selling links to others? How much authority does the page have? How many other natural and organic links are going to the page linking to you?

2. <u>Google Sandbox?</u> – Has the page in question suffered from a penalty? Is the page in Google's Sandbox?

iii. Age

1. <u>When was the domain first registered?</u> – Older domains tend to have more authority and trust. A weak relevancy signal looks at the date the domain was first

registered.

2. <u>When was the domain first indexed?</u> – A stronger relevancy signal comes from the date that the domain was first indexed by Google. Has it been two or more years or is it brand new?

3. <u>When does the domain expire?</u> – A Google patent reveals that the domain expiration date is a relevancy signal. Most spammy sites are only registered for one year in advance whereas "serious" domains are registered for years in advance.

iv. Domain

1. <u>Keywords in domain?</u> – Does the page's primary keyword exist in the domain? This isn't as strong of a relevancy signal as it was in the past, but it still holds importance.

2. <u>Keywords in subdomain?</u> – Does the page's keywords exist in the subdomain?

3. <u>Keywords as first word in domain?</u> – Is the keyword the first word in the domain or does it start the domain?

4. <u>Exact match domain (EMD)?</u> – Does the page's primary keyword match the domain name exactly?

5. <u>Domain history</u> – Has the domain switched ownership multiple times or has the traffic fallen off in peaks or has there been a steady and natural buildup in the domain over time?

6. <u>Public or private registration?</u> – Private registrations could be an

indication that the domain owner has something to hide.

7. <u>Country top-level domain extension (TLD)?</u> – Is this a top-level domain such as .US or .CA?

8. <u>Whois ownership specific data</u> – Who owns the domain name? Is it a real business?

9. <u>Parked domain?</u> – Is this just a parked domain?

10. <u>Domain Trustworthiness?</u> – How trustworthy is the domain linking to you? Have they built up trust with Google over time? Have they had any penalties?

v. Piracy

1. <u>DMCA complaints?</u> – Have there been DMCA complaints about the domain or page linking to you?

2. <u>IP Address flagged as SPAM?</u> – Has the IP address of the linking domain been flagged for SPAM or blacklisted?

vi. Relevancy

1. <u>Domain diversity on SERPs?</u> – The Bigfoot algorithm update helped to diversify domains on SERPs so that a single search wasn't wielding too many results from the same domain.

2. <u>Transactional searches for shopping-related queries?</u> – Searches that are using micro-data can now appear for shopping related queries. How relevant is your search when it comes to this?

3. Big brand relevancy? – Big brands tend to appear at the top of SERPs for certain short-tail keywords. This was part of the Vince algorithm update.

4. Brand name search text? – Does the search text involve a brand name? This is a moderate relevancy signal.

5. Brands with higher likes and shares on Facebook and Twitter? – Does the brand have a high number of likes and shares on Facebook and Twitter?

6. Image results? – Images can come before certain SERP listings on popular image searches.

7. Easter egg results? – These are moderate

hoaxes. For example, if you search with the word "askew" or "tilt," that will change the orientation of results. Similarly, Google might deliver games in its SERPs from time to time as well.

8. <u>Single-site results from brands with multiple SERP listings?</u> – If the search is for a brand-oriented keyword, Google's SERPs might bring up many listings from the same domain.

9. <u>Real business?</u> – Is this a real business? Is it a legitimate operation? This has an effect on relevancy.

10. <u>Verified brick-and-mortar location?</u> – Has the physical location been verified through a service like Google local?

11. <u>Tax-paying business?</u> – Is the business a tax paying business?

12. <u>Panda penalties?</u> – Has the domain suffered Panda penalties?

13. <u>Penguin penalties?</u> – Has the domain suffered Penguin penalties?

14. <u>Manual penalties?</u> – Has the domain suffered from manual Google penalties?

c. Social

i. **Social Reputation**

1. <u>Site reputation?</u> – What type of social reputation does the site have? Has it been reviewed or rated?

2. <u>Social media votes?</u> – Are there social media votes for the site?

3. <u>Social signal relevancy?</u> – How relevant are the social signals that are pointing to the site?

4. <u>Site-level social signals?</u> – Does the site have strong social signals? How many people shared and liked it?

ii. Online Reviews

1. <u>User reviews?</u> – Are there positive user reviews for the site?

iii. Social Media Shares

1. <u>Number of Tweets?</u> – How many Tweets does the site or page have?

2. <u>Authority of Tweet users?</u> – What's the authority of those tweeting? Do they have a large and active real following?

3. Number of Facebook shares? – How many Facebook shares does the site or page have?

4. Number of Facebook likes? – How many Facebook likes does the site's page have?

5. Authority of Facebook user accounts? – What's the authority of the Facebook user accounts that like and share the page?

6. Number of Pintrest Pins? – How many Pintrest Pins does the page have? How many does the site have in total to the domain?

7. Number of Google Plus Ones? – How many Google Plus Ones does the site have? How many does the page have?

8. <u>Authority of Google Plus users?</u> – What's the authority of the Google Plus users who've liked and shared that page or domain?

9. <u>Website has a Twitter profile with followers?</u> – Does the Website have a Twitter profile? Are there followers?

10. <u>Website has a Facebook profile with fans?</u> – Is there a Facebook page setup for the company with real fans?

11. <u>Official LinkedIn page for company?</u> – Does the company have a LinkedIn page?

12. <u>Employees listed on LinkedIn pages?</u>

13. <u>News media mentions of site?</u>

d. User-Specific

i. **Country or Region**

1. <u>Geo targeting search?</u> – Is there any country or geographic targeting that needs to be considered with the search? Things like top-level domains and region-specific data come into focus.

ii. **City or Locality**

1. <u>Locally applicable search?</u> – Does the listing apply to locally applicable search? How relevant is it for a local search?

iii. **History**

1. <u>Click-through-rate (CTR) for a keyword in searches where you relevantly appear in the results</u> – What's the CTR for that particular

keyword search?

2. <u>Click-through-rate for all keywords in searches where you relevantly appear in the results</u> – What's the CTR for all searches related to your site?

3. <u>Bounce rate of users visiting your site?</u> – Are they leaving the page without visiting other pages? Did they find the answer they were searching for or did they not like what they read? This is used in conjunction with time spent on the page.

4. <u>Exit rate of users visiting your site?</u> – What's the exit rate of users visiting that page from a SERP? Is the exit rate high or low? Are they visiting other pages?

5. <u>High direct traffic?</u> – Is

there a high level of direct traffic to the page or domain?

6. <u>High repeat traffic?</u> – Are users going back to certain links again and again? These sites are considered as higher quality by Google.

7. <u>Blocked websites?</u> – A signal used in Google's Panda, block sites were part of the user-experience. However, this is no longer part of Chrome.

8. <u>Google Toolbar data?</u> – Information is collected from Google's toolbar for user-specific searches. How much time are they spending on a page, and what other user-specific search factors are involved with that search?

9. <u>Time spent on site?</u> – A greater number would indicate higher quality of content. This data could then be used in subsequent searches.

10. <u>User's browsing history?</u> – What sites has the user visited in the past? Would that increase the relevancy of the page in question?

iv. Social

1. <u>Large number of comments and user interaction?</u> – Are there a large number of comments and user interaction about the shared links?

2. <u>Safe search?</u> – Does the user have safe search enabled? And does your site have any kind of profanity or adult content that would stop it from appearing?

3. <u>Google Plus circles?</u> — How many Google Plus circles are the users in who've shared the links?

10

ANALYTICS & TOOLS

Conducting your SEO work takes a significant amount of effort and work. As you've already witnessed in this book, there is an exhaustive and comprehensive set of rules, principles, methods, and techniques behind building trust and relevancy.

The only way that you can ensure that your time and your efforts aren't wasted is to enable a system for tracking and analyzing your SEO-related efforts. Of course, excel spreadsheets are an excellent way to stay organized for your on-page and off-page work, but it doesn't end there.

We must track and analyze, not only the Website's traffic, but also our position on the SERPs. Of course, you could opt for a slew of over-the-counter software provided by non-Google parties, but today it's simply not necessary.

Today, what you need are two primary tools that you need to help track your SEO Efforts:

1.   Google Analytics

2.   Google Webmaster Tools

You could also opt for the Google Tag Manager, but it's not an absolute necessity. For the time being, I would recommend setting up an account with both services if you haven't already done so. The analytics suite by Google is phenomenal and will provide you with a wide range of data.

Analytics will allow you to assess, not only the success of your SEO work away from the site, but also your work on the site. You can determine things like the average time spent on a page by visitors, the bounce rate, the exit rate, landing pages, and so on.

When you correlate this type of data across your site, you can get a clear indication whether or not people are finding your site, sticking around if your content is actually good, or even making successful conversions by filling out a form or completing a purchase.

Google's Webmaster Tools are also excellent because it gives you an avenue for determining which keywords are most often being used to find your site. Unfortunately, you can no longer do this very much through Google's Analytics since they've now made an almost complete transition to secured search.

Secured search, as you might already know, is Google's effort to ensure that all searches across all of its platforms are encrypted. For this reason, as time has gone on, Google Analytics has no longer displayed relevant keyword data for visitors arriving organically to your site.

In its place, Google Analytics now displays things like "(not set)" rather than an actual keyword. As you can imagine, this makes tracking and analyzing your SEO efforts much more difficult. That's where Google's Webmaster Tools come into play.

Webmaster Tools allow you to regain some of that insight into the keyword searches being performed by people arriving to your site. Although it's not 100% complete, Google is attempting to provide more transparency in this as time goes on.

Additionally, Webmaster Tools will tell you the number of times you appeared in search along with your SERP positioning for each keyword you were found relevantly for. This information is helpful to say the least, since it provides a scorecard of sorts that you can analyze over time.

What's important is to ensure that you have some system in place for tracking and analyzing your work. You'll also want to watch your trends over time, so you should record your data in some way. This doesn't have to take up enormous amounts of time, but time spent here will pay off.

Why record and track? Well, there's no better way to gauge your results. How are people finding your site? How much time are they spending there? What keywords are they using? You can find some of this data in historical format when using Webmaster Tools, but you should track what you can on a spreadsheet.

OTHER RESOURCES

Plenty of resources exit on the Web that will help to move your SEO educational career along its path. Hopefully, by this point, you now have a better understanding of what it takes to succeed in SEO. And I hope that I was able to drive home some of the more far-reaching concepts to you.

By now, you most likely understand the importance of high quality, unique content that adds value to people's lives. It really is at the basis of all that you will do on the Web. Getting really good at crafting excellent SEO keyword-centric content should be your primary concern.

To that effect, I would recommend conducting Google searches every day in areas that interest you and reading the top three listings on its SERPs. Give those pages a good analysis. Run those pages through the SEO Quake filter. What insight can you gain from them?

Reading and writing content will also help you to improve in SEO. Keep in mind that practice makes perfect. You can't get great at something without practicing it over and over again. If you're familiar with Malcolm Gladwell's 10,000-hour rule from his book, *Outliers*, then you know just what it takes to truly succeed at something.

The problem with SEO is that it doesn't happen overnight. Trust and relevancy are earned over time. As we've seen, the pace can be quickened, but it can't be unnaturally forced forward. So, we have to dig in our heels and simply do the work, it's that plain and simple.

But, now that you have some knowledge under your belt, you can get out there and actually focus on delivering high quality, unique content that delivers huge value. Practice marketing content, and possibly engaging in some more advanced SEO strategies over time.

It won't happen overnight, but it will happen over time as long as you stay committed and you don't give up.

R.L. ADAMS

THANK YOU

I hope that you enjoyed reading the material covered in this course. Hopefully, you've come to understand the ins-and-outs of the SEO industry far better, now.

Keep in mind that SEO takes work. It's an ever-evolving industry and it requires a level of expertise and maintenance over time. You simply can't set it and forget about it.

For that reason, I would hope that you continue your SEO education. Read, absorb, learn, and practice. Then, repeat. Over time, you become an expert at anything.

There will be frustrations and there will be upsets. But if you keep at it, then you will succeed with SEO, as you would with any other skill that you were resilient and committed to learning.

I would greatly appreciate if you would take a few moments to share your thoughts about this book by posting an online review. *Even one sentence would help.*

I put a lot of time and care into these books and I truly hope to deliver an enormous amount of value. And I hope that I've done that here for you.

Best of luck to you and God speed.

Made in the USA
Lexington, KY
24 July 2015